LOVE
GONE
WRONG

Steve.
- "For a friend"

Thomas A. White

LOVE
GONE
WRONG

**WHAT TO DO
WHEN YOU
ARE ATTRACTED
TO THE
WRONG PERSON
OVER AND
OVER**

THOMAS A. WHITEMAN, Ph.D., AND
RANDY PETERSEN

THOMAS NELSON PUBLISHERS
Nashville

Published in Nashville, Tennessee, by Oliver-Nelson Books, a division of
Thomas Nelson, Inc., Publishers, and distributed in Canada by Word Com-
munications, Ltd., Richmond, British Columbia.

The Bible version used in this publication is THE NEW KING JAMES
VERSION. Copyright © 1979, 1980, 1982, Thomas Nelson, Inc., Publishers.

Library of Congress Cataloging-in-Publication Data

Whiteman, Tom.
    Love gone wrong / Thomas A. Whiteman and Randy Petersen.
        p.   cm.
    ISBN 0-8407-9637-4 (pbk.)
    1. Relationship addiction—Religious aspects—Christianity.
    2. Interpersonal relations—Religious aspects—Christanity.
    I. Petersen, Randy. II. Title.
    BV4596.R43W55   1994
    248.4—dc20   93-23466
                                                                      CIP

Printed in the United States of America
1 2 3 4 5 6 — 99 98 97 96 95 94

CONTENTS

INTRODUCTION

Why would a woman stay with a man who abuses her?

Why do so many very competent single women seem to settle for men who appear to be so "beneath" them?

How can a man who has everything going for him—a good job, a fine home, a loving wife and children—have an affair that might jeopardize it all?

Why does a parent—whose job is to prepare a child for life outside the home—continue to baby a child well into adulthood and restrict the child's development as an independent person?

These may all be examples of *Love Gone Wrong*—or what we call *addictive relationships*, relationships driven by a compulsive urge rather than sacrificial love.

Is this just the latest entry in the Addiction-of-the-Month Club? Talk shows are booked solid with workaholics, spendaholics, food addicts, gambling addicts, and TV addicts. Are we now going to blame all our weaknesses on a new phantom illness—love addiction?

I believe that millions of individuals are walking around with addictive personalities, but they have never taken drugs or gotten drunk. Instead, these people will act out their addictive tendencies in more socially acceptable ways. And what could be more acceptable than "love"? Such people crave a fix from their lovers or fantasies just as surely as any substance abuser craves a fix from his or her drug of choice. By the way, in this book the word *lovers* refers to people who are in love; it does not necessarily imply a sexual relationship. As a Christian, I do not condone sexual relations outside of marriage, but as a Christian *counselor*, I deal with these real-life issues on a regular basis. In this book I have sought to handle this issue in an open and honest way, but I trust that no one will mistake my frankness for a flippant view of God's standard for our sexuality.

Have you ever said or thought the following?

- "I'll just die if I can't be with him."
- "If she leaves me, I'll do something drastic."
- "You are my everything. I would be nothing without you."

These words make for nice poetry or hit love songs, but in reality they smack of a relationship that is way out of balance. If you've said such things, you aren't necessarily in an addictive relationship, but you may want to investigate further just how dependent you are.

Don't get me wrong. This book is not anti-relationship. Healthy relationships are some of the best gifts God gives us—healing, restorative, pleasurable. But unhealthy relationships are disastrous. This book will help you identify danger signs, avoid or escape from bad relationships, and establish healthy relationship habits.

Many of the people I deal with in my counseling practice are single—divorced or never married. Thus, many of my examples have to do with romantic addictions in dating relationships. But unhealthy addictions can also occur in marriage, so I include a special chapter for that situation in which slightly different rules apply. Same-sex friendships and family relationships can also be troubled by addictive tendencies. Other chapters will focus on these areas.

No matter what your specific situation, most of the general principles of addictive relationships—how you got in and how to get out—will pertain to you. And that's the focus of the bulk of this book.

I first became aware of addictive relationships about five years ago as a counselor at Life Counseling Services in Paoli, Pennsylvania. I frequently encountered clients, usually women, who seemed to be making very poor choices in relationships. What confused me was that even when the clients knew what to look for in a relationship, and even when they were determined to hold out for a healthy partner, they inevitably repeated the same mistake by choosing someone who was all wrong for them.

I must admit my frustration in trying to help them. Week after week we went over the same principles, and each week they seemed even more determined to break off the addictive relationship and try once again to go it alone. But somehow they were never able to overcome the compulsive lure of the other person. I gradually concluded that sheer willpower was not enough.

I was struck by the similarities between the people and the drug addicts I had observed. Relationships were, for those women, their drug of choice.

I had observed the difficulties that substance abusers faced. Even when they knew that drug or alcohol use was tearing them apart, they seemed unable to overcome its viselike grip on their lives. The most effective method I found for overcoming the addictions was through a "cold turkey" inpatient treatment program, followed by close accountability through a support group or a sponsor.

When I heard the women talk about their destructive relationships and their inability to overcome the hold of another person on their lives, I began to realize that perhaps they needed similar treatment. We could not provide a thirty-day treatment program or a detox unit, but I was able to put together a support group of seven clients who were struggling with seemingly similar problems. The Group, as we called it, decided to meet two nights a week since they all felt that they needed close accountability and support.

But then I had a problem. What curriculum would the group use? What treatment method would work with such a group? I was unaware of any materials available for the specific needs. So I decided to adapt some material developed for persons recovering from other addictions. Much of the group was educational in nature, but there was also great benefit from our shared stories and the loving accountability that we brought each other from week to week.

Although this first support group served as the foundation for much of the material presented in this book, it has been supplemented over the past five years by seminars, additional support groups, and counseling with many individuals. I acknowledge their courage and determination in sharing their stories, and I am grateful that they decided to step forward and talk about the struggle and guilt that they have had to face in these difficult relationships.

The five case studies appear with the consent of the people involved. Still, I have changed all of the names and some of the details of the stories to protect people's identities. You should be aware that we are seeing the *other* characters in these people's lives *through their lenses,* which are biased. In truth, the others may not be as bad as they seem from these stories (there is another side to every story). I intend no judgment or criticism of them (their names and details are also changed). I merely seek to present lessons from the lives of these clients.

Other stories appear from time to time in the text. I have struggled to maintain both the confidentiality of the counseling office and my journalistic integrity. In some cases, I have developed composite characters, mixtures of people I have known or counseled. I feel sure that the mixing of details makes these people unrecognizable and thus preserves their privacy. However, the essential facts and the lessons learned are accurate.

As you read of the struggles of the men and women who contributed their stories to this book, I hope they will enlighten and inspire you. If you are suffering within an addictive relationship, these pages may give you the push you need to take a first step or two toward health.

Chapter One

THE GROUP

It is a hot and sticky July night. Seven people sit in a circle of chairs in my counseling office. We have engaged in some small talk as we gathered, but now we're all present, all seated, and the session has begun.

There is an awkwardness as heavy as the muggy air. I try to ease things with a friendly introduction. "You may wonder why I've called you here tonight. You don't know each other—yet. But each of you has spent some time talking with me about some difficult situations you're facing. As you'll soon see, some of your situations are amazingly similar. I thought it would be helpful to compare notes."

I don't want to force anyone to speak up, so I ask for a volunteer to go first. The silence returns. Suddenly, no one looks me in the eye. Then Dawn, perhaps because she's sitting next to me, clears her throat softly, takes an extra breath, and speaks.

"I was divorced about five years ago. Maybe I'm still not over it. Since then, I've been in four relationships. I guess you'd call them intimate relationships. It's hard for me to admit that because I'm . . . well . . . I'm a Christian. I really don't believe in being like that. But it's been really hard," she says.

1

Dawn takes a deep breath and continues, "Right now I'm seeing a man. I care a lot about him. I'm not sure what he thinks of me. He's married."

I ask some questions, guiding Dawn gently through her story. She grew up with an alcoholic father, and she maintains deep memories of longing for his unhindered affection. She married young, but that relationship soured soon after the honeymoon. She tried hard to make it work, "but apparently not hard enough," she whimpers.

The divorce had been his idea, a rejection that wounded her deeply. She sought healing in the arms of other men, landing in one unhealthy romance after another. She describes a chain of emotionally abusive, sometimes physically abusive, relationships. Yet she remained faithful in each one. The men "tired" of her, she explains. "I don't know what's wrong with me," she says coldly, "but it didn't take any of them very long to find out."

Like several of the group members, Dawn had been a Christian since childhood. It had been a rocky road for her. Each new relationship began with a solid conviction about sexual restraint, but in the heat of passion and the fire of self-doubt, those convictions melted. Dawn hated herself for "giving in" so easily, but she tried to justify it in various ways. After all, since her divorce, she was "damaged goods" anyway. And she would never get the love she needed from men without giving something in return.

Of the married man she's seeing, she says, "I liked being with him. He made me feel very special. At first I thought it could just be a good friendship. Whatever else I was, I was not a home wrecker. Well, I guess I didn't have to worry about that because there is no way he is going to leave his wife for me. I'm just a side dish. And, yes, of course it got romantic, and it got physical. I got in so deep that now I can't get out. And I admit, there's something exciting about it. Something bad. I hate that and I love it at the same time."

Dawn glances over at me, as if I am judging her presentation. "I know I have to stop seeing him," she says slowly, articulating each word. "I know that. But he's . . . like . . . inside of me. I need him."

As I look around the circle, I see some nods of encouragement. These people know what she's talking about. They've been there. Some, though, are still staring at the floor. Maybe Dawn's story hit too close to home.

"Thank you," I say to Dawn. "And thank you for having the courage to speak first. It's not easy, I know. I'm wondering if we can just go around the circle. Margie, would you like to tell us about your situation?"

MARGIE'S STORY

Margie is in her mid-twenties; she's an energetic young woman. "I was hoping you'd go the other direction," she says wryly, then a smile crosses her face. "But, okay, I'll go. What do you want to know?"

"Why are you here?"

"Because my boyfriend's busy tonight." Margie's face is like the sky on a partly cloudy day. Her natural energy normally radiates through her facial expressions, but then a cloud passes, and all turns dark. "That's really true," she adds with dark cynicism. "And that's really why I'm here."

Margie describes her boyfriend as "a ladies' man." He treats her like a princess, but she wonders how many other princesses are in his court. They've never been able to talk about it because "I'm afraid of saying something dumb and losing him," she says. "Whenever we talk about anything even remotely resembling commitment or the future or marriage especially, he clams up or changes the subject, or I won't see him for a week."

There are mumbles of recognition from the other women in the circle. They know the symptoms.

I ask Margie about her upbringing. She reveals that she grew up without a father in her home and she was probably overdependent on her mother. She dated a lot as a teenager and as a young adult, but she found that several steady relationships quickly went out of balance. "I needed the guy more than he needed me," she says. "That always causes problems. And I guess now it's the same old story."

Her sunny look comes out again briefly. "In a lot of ways I'm lucky, I guess. My boyfriend is a really great guy. He takes me to very expensive restaurants and exciting places. Believe me, I've dated a lot of toads whose idea of a night on the town is a hockey game and a few beers afterward. I should count my blessings."

Then the clouds roll in. "But lots of times he is mysteriously unavailable. Some weekends, he's just gone. No explanation. I keep hoping he's an international spy or something, but I know he's got to be seeing someone else. And that really gets me down. I called his answering machine thirty times one weekend. That's all I did. I sat at home and moped and punched the buttons on the phone. I know I should stand up for my rights . . . be strong. But I'm really afraid he'll go. And what will I do then? I figure a nice date once in a while is better than no date at all."

JOY'S STORY

Joy speaks next. She proudly proclaims to the group that she has had only one true love in her whole life. She started dating her husband in ninth grade and finally married him while they were in college. They have been married about ten years. "And now," Joy says, her voice cracking, "we're separated."

There are a few empathetic moans from the group. Dawn digs out a tissue from her purse and offers it to Joy, who just clutches it in her hand.

"My husband has been seeking a divorce about three years now," Joy continues, "but I've said no. Maybe I'm crazy, but I believe that God will bring him back to me. I still love him very much in spite of everything, and I don't see how he can walk away from that. And we have three children."

Young children. Joy is barely thirty. The oldest child is seven. As Joy speaks of the difficulty of raising the kids on her own, her anger shows through. She is mild-mannered, but a fury is raging inside her. She states, "My husband is presently living with someone else, and he says he's giving me all the child-support money he can afford, but I know he's spending a lot on her. That really bothers me. I mean, where is his responsibility? It's with me and the children . . . not with her."

"If it hurts so much," asks Dawn, "why don't you just let him go?" It's not an attack, just a question. And as soon as she asks it, Dawn knows there's no good answer. Why don't you just let him go? Each woman in the group wrestles with that issue. It's far easier to say it than to do it.

"Lots of my friends ask me that," Joy responds. "They say I should move on with my life . . . get the divorce. But I love him. Don't you see? There are promises there, promises we have made to each other. He may break his word, but that doesn't mean I can break mine. I believe in the power of love. I believe in the power of God. I must remain faithful. I don't know what God is doing here, to test me or what, but I have to keep loving my husband. I still believe that someday he will see the error of his ways and come back."

LAURIE'S STORY

After a few moments of silence, all eyes turn to Laurie, next in line. She is in her mid-forties, impeccably made up and dressed to kill. Come to think of it, I have never seen her, in any of our sessions, in anything less than the height of business fashion. She seems the essence of the assertive modern woman.

"Never date anyone you work with," she says boldly. "Never. Never. Never!"

"Is that the voice of experience?" Margie quips.

Laurie looks over to her and nods slowly. "I'm here because I broke my own rules. I knew better. Ten months ago, my boss started showing a personal interest in me, and I should have waved a stop sign at him right away. But I kind of liked the attention. And he paid a lot of attention to me—seven hours a day, five days a week. Maybe he wore me down, I don't know. But we started dating, casually at first. Then . . . uh . . . not so casually."

The relationship is bad, Laurie says, and she knows she needs to get out of it. But she doesn't know how. "He's a really sexy guy, but he's a real jerk, too. I don't know why God allows the two qualities to go together so very often, but this guy's at the top of the list in both categories." She details how he has taken advantage of her in the workplace and in private. He has used her devotion to help him professionally, and he has pushed her to surrender to him sexually in ways she had never intended. Now she feels miserable and trapped.

"Every day I think, *Okay, this is the day it ends.* But then I see him, and I lose my nerve. He has this power over me. I don't know how to say it. I *want* him. I want to be with him all the time."

Laurie admits to the group that she has been married and divorced twice and she has no desire to marry again. "I swore I would never again let a man have that kind of power over me," she states. "But here I am, unable or unwilling to get this man out of my life, out of my heart, even though I know it's all wrong."

DAVID'S STORY

David and I are the only men present. With a flippant comment about "equal time," I invite him to speak. I assume he must feel some discomfort at the male bashing that's gone on so far, but he shows no hesitancy.

"I guess I'm the guy you're all talking about," he smiles. "The jerk, the ladies' man, the one who 'takes advantage.' Are men really that bad?"

"They're worse," says Laurie.

"Yeah," Margie adds. "You should hear what we'd say if you guys weren't here!"

Tension-easing laughter fills the room. This is good. The group is working as it should. The initial awkwardness has worn off. Some therapeutic connections are being made.

"Seriously," David resumes, "I *am* like that, like those other guys, though I'm not proud to admit it. And I guess in some ways I'm like you. Maybe it will help to get a male perspective."

"Fire away," I say.

"I'm thirty-three years old and single . . . never married. That means I've had a lot of years of dating. I'd say there have been nine or ten pretty intense relationships . . . steady relationships . . . in that time and a handful of minor ones. Most of them fit the same pattern."

David goes on to say how it started with his first girlfriend, back in high school. He had "worshiped" the girl from afar for over a year until finally she returned his interest and they began dating. The reality didn't match the fantasy. After a few months, he broke up with her.

David's face shows pain even now as he retells it: "I hated doing that. She was a fine person, but I just didn't want her anymore. That sounds cruel, doesn't it? But that's the truth of it. And the worst thing is that I've done the same thing again and again. I idolize a woman. Then if I do start a relationship with her, I'm disappointed that she's not the perfect woman I wanted."

"But no one's perfect," says Dawn.

"I know," David replies. "And maybe I don't mean exactly perfect but perfectly fulfilling for me. You know? I'm looking for a woman who will be right for me, someone who will strengthen my strengths and make up for my failings. She doesn't need to be perfect, but she needs to be right for me."

David rehearses the pattern of intense pursuit, euphoric conquest, and ultimate disillusionment. He obviously regrets the pain he has caused along the way, but he explains, "That's the way I am. I have high standards." As I prod him with questions, he reveals that his "standards" are astronomical—looks, intelligence, humor, spirituality, creativity—"the bionic woman," as Margie jokes.

What's more, David says he feels an "emptiness" that he expects this wonder woman to fill. "I keep looking . . . all the time," he says. "It's like my major goal in life, to find the right woman and love her like crazy. And every room I walk in to, I think maybe she will be there. I know that's corny, but I'm always checking out every woman I see. Will she measure up? Will she be the one?"

"What about this room?" asks Laurie, sitting beside him. "Have you been checking *us* out?"

David looks suddenly shy, his eyes darting along the floor. "Well, to be honest, yes."

I seize the moment. "That's honest. Thank you, David. Remember, we're not here to judge each other. We're here to share our situations, to compare notes. And I believe we're up to Ginnie."

GINNIE'S STORY

Ginnie is the most soft-spoken person in the group. There is a deep beauty in her dark eyes, but she has done nothing to display it. She is dressed plainly, and she wears little makeup. She peers at the others through large glasses that seem to cover half her face. Actually, I was surprised she showed up. I knew the group session might be difficult for her, but it might also provide sorely needed support.

"Well, I've never been married," she begins softly, "but I've had a number of . . . I guess you'd call them relationships. I've been hurt a lot. And maybe I've hurt others. My problem is . . ." She stops for a moment and looks straight at me, as if for prompting. I gaze back with friendly encouragement. She is going to have to tell her own story.

"Well, the reason I'm here is that I get really physical with men really fast . . . too fast. And then it's no good anymore. They don't want me or I don't want them or I don't really know how to turn that into love. It feels so great for a moment. I mean, you're in bed and it feels like it's forever. But it never is."

Ginnie is suddenly very self-conscious. She folds her arms across her chest and looks down. "I'm sorry. I shouldn't have said that."

There are several whispers of "No!" from the group, and I voice their support. "No, Ginnie, I'm glad you mentioned that. I think a number of people here can identify with those feelings." I am pleased that she spoke up as much as she did. From our counseling sessions, I am aware of Ginnie's ongoing struggle. Though she is a Christian and would like to live a chaste life, she has never been able to maintain that for more than a few months. Then it's out to the bars again for a series of one-night stands. Whenever a relationship seems to be taking hold, she does something to sabotage it. I suspect that the idea of a lasting relationship scares her to death, even though it inhabits her dreams.

I also know from our private sessions that Ginnie was sexually abused by her father. The only time she could get her father to pay attention to her was when he would come to her bedroom at night. That was how she learned to relate to men.

Realizing the depth of Ginnie's troubles, I know we won't solve them all tonight. I let her off the hook, moving on to Karen, a woman of about thirty-five. Karen is the last one in the circle.

KAREN'S STORY

"I've been divorced about two years," Karen says. "It was a horrible marriage while it lasted. I was verbally and emotionally abused for years. And I didn't really realize it at the time. I just took it. It makes me mad now when I think about it."

"So what made you get the divorce?" asks Laurie.

"I found out he was having an affair with another woman. That was the last straw. It was a total shock, and I just couldn't deal with it. We separated almost immediately, and the divorce was fairly easy. But you know, it was the strangest thing. Once the divorce was final, I cried for three days. I was finally free from this . . . this monster, and I was grieving like it was the end of the world."

Karen goes on to talk about the relationships that came later. She felt a void in her life. In a way, she needed someone to take her husband's place. And she found one. She describes a current relationship with a man who also treats her poorly. He takes her for granted, always calls her at the last minute, and never takes her anyplace that would cost him more than a few dollars, even though he has plenty of money. He continually promises her an increased commitment and eventual marriage, and yet he acts more and more distant. When Karen confronts him on some of these issues, he claims she is nagging and tells her to "get off his case."

"For about six months now," she says, "I've been trying to break up with him. And every time I do, every time I think it's finally over, he calls me and sweet-talks me into giving it another try. I'm so torn. I get angry, and I say, 'We can't go on like this!' But deep inside, I need him. I miss him if we're not together. I really can't stand to be unconnected to him."

"Can't live with him, can't live without him," says Margie. "I know the feeling." The others nod their assent.

COMMON GROUND

As you can see, there are major similarities in these people's stories. That's why I called the group together. It is common for people to isolate themselves in such situations. They feel that they possess a major personality flaw and they are all alone.

The fact is that millions make the same kinds of mistakes. That doesn't mean it's not a problem. That does mean the person is not abnormal. And getting together with others and comparing notes can be extremely therapeutic.

Let's take a look at the similarities of the people in our group.

1. They are intensely drawn to a person or a particular kind of relationship, even to the point of irrationality. Such an addiction can share many aspects of drug or alcohol addiction. Their "drug of choice" is a particular relationship.

2. They seem unable to break the unhealthy cycle of relating. They try to break up but can't. They divorce one jerk and begin dating another. They repeat the same patterns, even though they know how bad the patterns are.

3. They seek personal fulfillment in a particular person or relationship. Each one in the group shows a lack of self-esteem, some more than others. All of them reach out for a "missing piece" that will make them whole again.

This, I believe, is the addiction of the nineties. The sexual revolution, the divorce epidemic, the technological isolation of individuals—all have contributed to a situation in which we long for healthy relationships, but we have no idea how to get them. Our relationships are often twisted and unbalanced, beset by absurdly high expectations or low self-image. We are more aware than ever of our need for someone else, but too often we build up that need to messianic proportions that can be met only by, well, by the Messiah.

Virtually anyone can get involved in an addictive relationship—it doesn't matter whether someone is single or married, male or female, old or young, Christian or non-Christian, New Ager or staunch fundamentalist. A person can be addicted to a husband or wife, boyfriend or girlfriend, parent or child, close friend or new acquaintance. The addiction can be fairly benign or obsessive and dangerous. In any case, we need to recognize relationship addiction as addiction and treat it accordingly.

Although recent movies such as *Fatal Attraction* depict the dark side of obsessive relationships, popular culture often describes healthy relationships in addictive terms. We talk about being "crazy" about someone, implying that there's something wonderfully irrational about the attraction. If I "Can't Smile Without You," that's supposed to be a testimony of true love, not of dangerous attachment. When the Stylistics crooned "You Are Everything," few of us thought about the problems of exalting a relationship to impossible levels. That's what love is supposed to be about, right?

Don't get me wrong. Love is great. And I'm not proposing some sort of coldly rational matchmaking system. But music, movies, TV shows, and books often tell us, "You are nothing if you aren't in love with someone. Then you have to be totally agog about this person, defying everything that makes sense, just to be with this person." That kind of thinking plays well on the airwaves, on the screen, and on the printed page, but in real life it can lead to warped relationships.

Human love is a powerful thing. Ultimately, it _is_ a matter of two people giving their lives to each other, two people becoming one unit. But it needs to be balanced (_both_ need to give) and healthy. When it's healthy, love builds up the lovers; it does not consume them.

So let's take a second look at the nature of addictive relationships before we tackle some of the variations on the theme.

Intense attraction, to the point of irrationality

This kind of love hurts. It consumes a person. We talk of being lovesick, longing for a person. In David's case, it is a temporary thing. He longs for a particular image of a woman he likes, but the reality never matches up. And Margie continues to crave a solid relationship with her "ladies' man" boyfriend, though she realizes he will probably never be able to provide that.

In cases of such intense attraction, we feel that we must hang on to the person or keep pursuing the prize in spite of the pain involved. We begin to sacrifice other relationships or to neglect aspects of our lives to maintain these unpromising or unhealthy relationships. And so the objects of our affection begin to gain control over our lives. We become dependent on the brief highs in the relationship, even though obtaining or maintaining these highs becomes harder and harder.

Also, the objects of our affection sometimes realize the effect they have on us, and they milk it for all it's worth. Notice how several women in our circle bemoan the attitudes of the men they clung to. As David put it once in a session with me, "Men may be jerks, but women are stupid . . . stupid for letting men be jerks." David acknowledges that it can work the other way, too. More than once, a woman has played around with his heart precisely because he allowed her to do so.

Strong love can be wonderful. But especially when it is not returned, it can be dangerous. Such intense attraction quickly throws a relationship out of balance. And many other difficulties follow.

Inability to break the unhealthy cycle of relating

The cocaine addict can reach a point where he hates what he's doing. The highs aren't so high; his habit is expensive and dangerous; it's ruining his life. But he's hooked. He can't get out, even though he recognizes how unhealthy it is.

With drugs and alcohol and some other addictions, there is a physical element. Body chemistry has changed, and withdrawal brings a host of physical symptoms. Relationship addiction does not have the same chemical hook, but the emotional hooks are powerful indeed. Virtually all of our group members want to get out of unhealthy relationships or to change their patterns of relating—and they just can't do it on their own. That's why they have come for counseling. They have sacrificed principles, convictions, friends, and self-respect to keep the unhealthy beast alive.

What amazes others as well as us is that even when we are quite aware of how wrong the relationship is, we seem unable or unwilling to give it up. We gripe to our friends but ignore their advice. We tolerate treatment that we swore we would never put up with, and we become miserable. Even if we seek professional help, we often discard the advice that we just spent our hard-earned dollars to hear. Addictive relationships are rooted in deep needs and can require deep therapy.

Devoted relationships are great. It's good to be loyal. But there's a major problem when you recognize that a relationship is unhealthy and a substantial part of you wants to get out of it, but you just can't.

Personal fulfillment sought in a particular person or relationship

Why do we act so irrationally? Because the fear of being all alone is greater than the pain of the relationship. "A bad relationship is better than no relationship at all," we figure. (Isn't that essentially what Margie just said?) This notion implies that by ourselves, we are unfulfilled, unworthy, and unhappy.

Many people feel that there's something missing in their lives.

And as we've seen, our popular culture has romanticized that: "You're Nobody Till Somebody Loves You." Romance takes on almost religious proportions. We are supposed to find the meaning of life in sex or romantic love. It's ironic, but not unusual, that the gospel song "Love Lifted Me" was reborn some years ago as a pop love song: "When nothing else could help, love lifted me." If that's God's love, that's a religious affirmation; if that's the love of a good person, that seems to put the person in the place of God. (More recently, Amy Grant's crossover hit "Love Will Find a Way" had the same double meaning.)

Once again, don't get me wrong. Romantic love *is* a beautiful, mysterious thing. It can lift a suffering soul. But too many people are searching for *ultimate* meaning in finite relationships. Their whole identity, their reason for living, is tied up in the affections or approval of another human being. These are religious issues. It is proper to seek ultimate meaning in God. Otherwise, people are bound to be disappointed.

Some scholars consider idolatry a root problem of addiction. Addicts put the "fix" (whatever that may be) in the place of God—worship it, serve it, depend on it, define themselves by it. As Gerald May writes in *Addiction and Grace*, "Spiritually, addiction is a deep-seated form of idolatry. The objects of our addictions become our false gods. These are what we worship, what we attend to, where we give our time and energy, *instead of love*. Addiction, then, displaces and supplants God's love as the source and object of our deepest true desire."

To some extent, human love does fulfill us. It can make us better people. It can be an outgrowth of divine love, and sometimes it can lead us to God. Certainly, the Bible depicts marriage as a picture of God's relationship with humans and the relationship within the Godhead. And many of us know folks who have found themselves by hooking up with the right person.

But you can place absurd expectations on human relationships. And that's dangerous. You don't really find yourself in a relationship. You find yourself in yourself—perhaps in the context of a relationship. Don't go looking for your soul in someone else's eyes.

Chapter Two

TYPES OF ADDICTIVE RELATIONSHIPS

It's no surprise that our sex-crazy culture celebrates relationship addiction in song. One recent hit described a person who was addicted to the point of being totally out of control—physically and emotionally. The popular refrain advises, "You might as well face it, you're addicted to love." Oh, to be free of any moral restraint. Oh, to be able to indulge all passion. Oh, to escape into a never-never land without responsibility. And of course, it's an ultimate fantasy to be with a sex partner who has no will, who exists only for your pleasure, isn't it? It makes sense that the singer who popularized the song "Addicted to Love" appears on the video with a cadre of women dressed exactly alike—tight dresses, slicked-back hair, and high heels. They are human sex dolls, with no individuality, no personality, no will.

That's addiction for you. For the addict in the thrall of an addiction, all of life boils down to one thing—the fix. Whether that's cocaine, whiskey, or a date on Saturday night, that becomes the focus of life. Nothing else matters. No one else matters. The addict depersonalizes everyone, including herself. The addict becomes a fix-seeking machine.

Can an addiction to a relationship—to a person—be depersonalizing? Yes. The relationship addict tends to replace the real person with an image, a false ideal of the person he adores. Addiction skews the vision of reality. Ironically, the person who so desperately seeks wholeness in a relationship actually prevents whole relationships from developing because of these false images.

When we talk about relationship addiction, we must define three major types. They may look the same, and they share many symptoms, but the objects of desire are quite different.

"LOVE" ADDICTION

Some people are just in love with being in love. They find themselves in a series of budding romances that somehow fail to pan out. The actual relationship is usually too difficult to maintain, once the euphoria of the romantic discovery has concluded. In some cases, the love addict demeans herself in an effort to revive the fading feeling. A wife may allow a husband to have affairs, to ignore her, to insult her, or even to abuse her—all in the hope that he will someday love her again.

Dawn could be considered a love addict. You remember her as the first one to speak up in the group. She was divorced five years earlier, and she experienced a series of painful relationships since then.

In private counseling, she told me she had never "been without someone" since the ninth grade. She was driven by the belief that someone out there would finally fulfill her and love her perfectly. The marriage had been promising but then deeply disappointing. Now she has found that exciting love in an affair with a married man—but in the back of her mind she knows it, too, will end in disappointment and pain.

David, the lone male in the group, also seems addicted to the pursuit of a perfect love. While this type of addiction is much more prevalent in women, it also exists with men.

Like Dawn, David is looking for fulfillment in a romantic relationship. A million movies, TV shows, and paperback novels promote the idea that romance brings fulfillment. As with most dangerous ideas, it is partly true. Go back to Adam and Eve and you have the "missing rib" idea, that we are lacking something until we find the missing piece. "The two shall become one flesh," which seems to imply that each person is worth only one-half.

That's where the problem exists. There's nothing wrong with seeking a loving relationship in which you find a certain fulfillment. But it gets dangerous when you *depend* on that relationship to *make you a full person.* A good loving relationship is the merger of two *whole* people. One plus one equals one. Let's not deal with fractions. (And by the way, the Bible regularly affirms the value of individuals and even recommends singleness for those who can manage it. It would be wrong for us to draw "fractional" inferences from the relationship of Adam and Eve.)

Addictions are built on a too-low opinion of oneself and a too-high opinion of the object of one's attraction. Dawn, of course, has a low view of herself. She is willing to put up with all sorts of mistreatment because she figures she isn't worth anything better. She draws her personal value from the men in her life—even when they beat her up.

David shows us the other side. His self-image is fairly healthy, but he has built an idol of the Perfect Woman. Fueled by magazine layouts and rock videos, his mind has generated an image of the woman who will fulfill his life. He keeps pursuing women who seem to have some of the desired traits, but he becomes disappointed when they don't measure up to his fantasy.

While he is in pursuit, David can act much the same way Dawn does. He does not have to deal with physical abuse, but he says he's been "used" by several women he was temporarily devoted to—stood up, taken advantage of, insulted. He allowed it to happen because he was still in the pursuit mode. He had not yet determined that she was *not* the One, so he would endure anything to keep her. Ironically, once he did win her affection, he would soon realize her shortcomings and ease out of the relationship.

SEX ADDICTION

Sex addiction can be personal or impersonal. Many in our society, mostly men, have become addicted to pornography in various forms. I would characterize it as an impersonal addiction since it focuses on the individual's sexual pleasure, usually through masturbation. While it does involve other people—models, actors, prostitutes—it does not generally involve an ongoing relationship with these people. For that reason it lies beyond the scope of this book. (I would, however, recommend the excellent work by Patrick Carnes, *Out of the Shadows*.)

For many others, men and women alike, sex addiction is played out in personal relationships. They use people for their own sexual compulsions. And it must also be said that pornography addiction has devastating effects on the marriages and the families of the addicts as well. As much as the users of pornography seek to isolate the compulsion, it spills over to the rest of life and fouls relationships.

Sex addiction is, on the surface, a quest for pleasure. But it can also be a quest for power or a method of self-sabotage. As with other "drugs," the desire for sex takes people further and further in their quest for a greater and greater high. Addicts find that the old pornography doesn't please them anymore, that they must indulge in new (sometimes dangerous or illegal) activities to attain the desired level of exhilaration and sexual release.

Often the pleasure is mingled with a sense of power. A man "conquers" a woman when he gets her into bed. A woman "controls" a man by tempting him into sexual relations. For some, it is the only power they have or the only power they consider important. Often late bloomers blossom into promiscuity. Their self-image was stamped in junior high or high school as "ugly duckling," "nerd," or "undesirable." They may spend the rest of their lives trying to prove how wrong those labels were. How? By flaunting their newfound desirability. By seducing every member of the opposite sex they can. Each new seduction is a triumph over the naysayers of their youth.

I know a very successful young man who is well respected in his business and in his community. You would think he'd be very happy with where he is and where he's going. But there are two areas of his life where he "failed" during high school. Though he was valedictorian and a popular student, he still regrets that he never succeeded at sports and with girls. So now what does he do? He plays softball, volleyball, tennis, and basketball with a vengeance, often risking injury to prove that he can excel, even in his thirties. And still single, he keeps dating the prettiest (and youngest) girls he can, even if they're all wrong for him. Sex for him is a conquest. He engages in high-risk dating—going out with women with questionable pasts. Once his conquest is complete, he moves on to new territory. His profile fits that of many sex addicts. For them, it's not the sex act itself but a meaning they attach to it. Sex is a victory, a vote of confidence, an emblem of power.

For Ginnie, from our group, sex is love. As I mentioned earlier, the only affection she got from her father was incestuous. And so she continues to attach love to sex. She exhibits all the symptoms of love addiction, except she seeks it through sex. And based on her story, she seems to be terrified by the thought that love could be anything more than sex. Whenever a sexual relationship threatens to become more than that—whenever it moves in the direction of love—she kills it. Though she yearns to be loved, true love is uncharted terrain for her, and it scares her to death.

For some others, and possibly Ginnie, too, sex is a form of self-sabotage. These people have deep feelings of self-hate. They believe themselves unworthy of love. This belief often results from childhood abuse. Sex is generally considered dirty, and so their sexual promiscuity is a way of playing in the mud. They find an odd sense of justice in their behavior. They punish themselves for being bad by being bad. They know sex without love is demeaning and painful, but they feel they don't deserve anything better.

I just saw a TV report on a young woman who seemed to be something like this. The daughter of a famous actor, she became a stripper and then an actress in a pornographic film. She knew her behavior hurt her parents and her husband and even herself, but she seemed to be driven to continue it. Her reported conversations indicate that she thought very poorly of herself, but she delighted in the shame she brought to her famous father through her behavior. Ultimately, she committed suicide, giving herself a death sentence for her sins.

That's an extreme case, to be sure. Most sex addicts are not nearly as public about it. In fact, many manage to keep it private until it grows out of control. They learn to lead double lives, indulging their addiction and carrying on seemingly normal lives.

At the request of the courts, I counseled Frank. He had been arrested for breaking into a woman's home at night and stealing her underwear. Since it was his first arrest, he was let off fairly easily. The police called him a weirdo and several other choice names, but the judge knew Frank needed serious counseling as well as punishment.

To all appearances, Frank was no weirdo. He had a good job, a wife, and two children. Considered a very moral person, he was a Sunday school teacher in my church. But obviously, Frank had another life—a secret life that no one else, not even his family, knew about.

Frank grew up in an alcoholic home. He swore he would never drink, and as far as I know, he kept that vow. However, his inherited addictive tendencies came out in other ways. When he was a teenager, it was compulsive masturbation. As a young man, he sought a greater high, so he turned to pornography. He felt very convicted each time he acted out, and he prayed to God to take away his lustful thoughts.

During that time, he had a steady girlfriend, but he never touched her sexually because he was afraid of what he might do.

He also never discussed his problem with her because he was afraid she would reject him and his sinful ways.

Eventually, Frank reasoned that his struggle stemmed from sexual frustration. Several friends told him that he just needed to "score" with someone and he would feel much better. But he clung to his Christian convictions, believing that sexual relations with someone outside marriage would be wrong. But what about sex within marriage? Surely that would solve his problem, he figured. After all, the Bible teaches that "it is better to marry than to burn" (1 Cor. 7:9). He was obviously burning with lust, but marriage would make that problem go away. He could have a normal sex life.

At first it worked. For the first several months the marriage was a solution, but he couldn't help noticing that his sex drive was far stronger than that of his new wife. Still, being married was far better than living with the guilt of the pornography and excessive masturbation.

But soon Frank began to masturbate again. He was disappointed with himself because he assumed that all of his sexual needs would be met by his wife. Yet he felt that he pushed her enough already to have sex a couple of times a week, and he did not feel comfortable pushing her any more. So he decided to go back to his old pattern of pornography and masturbation. That time he felt less guilt—"At least I'm not having an affair or hurting anyone."

But soon the pornography grew mundane, and masturbation seemed humiliating. He needed something more, he thought, a real woman. Once again, his strong convictions would not allow him to act on his thoughts. Instead, he fantasized about women he knew and sought some connection with them.

One woman in particular became an obsession. He eventually followed her home, and he began a sexual ritual of returning after dark to watch her through her window while he imagined having sex with her.

As with all of his attempts to satisfy a burning desire for more and more sexual excitement, Frank felt compelled to graduate to other women, then strangers, each time getting closer and closer without them ever knowing he was there. He began to call them and make obscene comments, climb trees to get closer looks, and enter their homes while they were away. With each new phase the excitement grew, but his desire for greater connection also grew. Each risk he took heightened his fulfillment but, eventually, led to greater risks.

Frank's behavior became more and more self-destructive. The breaking-and-entering charge put an end to the cycle, at least for a time. The woman was obviously scared half to death to discover a strange man in her room, going through her personal things. But for Frank, the woman had been his obsession for many months. When he saw how terrified she was, he was gripped with guilt. Somehow he had fantasized that their attraction was mutual.

Fortunately, Frank was caught. What would he have progressed to next? How far would his addiction have taken him? We don't know the answers to these questions in Frank's case, but our newspapers are filled with the stories of other sex addicts. We can see how far their addictions have led. Families have been torn apart, careers ruined, minds twisted.

But perhaps the greatest—and most common—destruction that sex addiction causes is the destruction of sexual satisfaction. Lost in a world of pornography, Frank could not be happy with his wife. She did not measure up to his fantasies. And so what should have been a beautiful thing, the expression of marital love through sexual intimacy, was poisoned.

A key word here is *attachment*. An addict attaches certain desirable qualities to a particular relationship or activity. These things then become fused together in the addict's mind. As we've seen, some people attach love to sex. So not only do they mistakenly feel loved when they're having sex, but they tend to feel unloved when they're not having sex. For some, power or control or self-worth is fused to their sexual behavior. That becomes the only time they can feel powerful, in control, or worth something. In Frank's case, as with many sex addicts, excitement was attached to pornography and voyeurism. And his compulsions removed the excitement from the rest of his life.

ADDICTION TO A PERSON

Person-addiction is a matter of attaching one's well-being to a specific person. It's not being in love with love or being driven by sexual desires, though it may exhibit some of the same symptoms. In the other relationship addictions we've considered, the addict reduces all of life to a status, an emotion, or an activity. With person-addiction, it's all wrapped up in that special person: "If I don't see Bob today, I'll die."

When Bob is away, she feels desperately alone and out of control. When the object of her devotion is present, the world revolves around him: "It does not matter what I think, what I feel, or what I want. I just want to make Bob happy." This is *emotional dependency*, and it can be dangerous.

Once again, our popular ideas of romance feed this dependency. When I was a kid, the Stylistics were singing, "You are everything, and everything is you." That was no Hindu hymn; it was a love song. We regularly express our love in such lofty terms.

But if "you are everything," what am I? How do I fit into this picture? The person-addict says, "I don't." He loses a sense of self while giving total devotion to the other, which makes for an unbalanced relationship. In the worst cases, the addicted partners endure terrible abuse but keep going back for more. They have no self-dignity to preserve. They cannot imagine living without their lovers/tormentors. They are convinced they would never be loved by anyone else—nor would they want to be.

This tendency is especially dangerous in Christian marriages. The Bible teaches submission in marriage. Many men use this teaching as a reason to lord it over their wives, but that was never Christ's idea of good leadership. Many women feel it's their Christian duty to "lose themselves" in a marriage—they *belong* to their husbands, and the husbands, in turn, treat their wives as possessions. In this atmosphere, a wife may become addicted to her husband in an unhealthy way.

But that's a skewed view of Scripture. Yes, the Bible teaches submission, but it also calls on husbands to love their wives "as Christ also loved the church and gave Himself for her" (Eph. 5:25). The giving goes both ways. Yes, the wife belongs to her husband, but the husband also belongs to his wife. "The two shall become one flesh," the Bible says. But for too many, that "one flesh" is the husband's. The truth of it is that there is a new entity in which both members are full partners.

I'm not talking about headship and who makes decisions and all of that. That's for another book. But I am saying that the Bible does not promote lopsided relationships in which one partner becomes addicted to the other. That is not good for anyone. Christ's command to "love your neighbor as yourself" carries this assumption: the best love we can offer anyone springs from a solid acceptance of ourselves.

Joy is a perfect example of person-addiction. As she explained to the group, she is hanging on to a husband who wants a divorce. She has been with him since childhood. While she acknowledges that the healthier thing might be to let him go and to start over, she does not know how to live without him.

But marriage isn't the only place we find person-addiction. Dating relationships can also develop in that direction, as we see with Margie and Laurie. Margie has found the perfect man—or so she thinks. The trouble is, some other women have found him, too. He is a ladies' man, dating around with no immediate desire to settle down. The relationship is lopsided. Margie is crazy about him, ready to mortgage heart and soul for his exclusive affections. But obviously, he isn't that far along in his affection for her. She fears (probably correctly) that if she presses the issue, she'll chase him away. So she stews in her addiction, happy for the few moments she can get and miserable without him. And apparently, he has learned the rules of this game: he holds all the cards; she will be there for him when he's ready.

In Laurie's case, the "rules" are even more one-sided. Laurie is addicted to her boss, who is "really sexy" and "a real jerk."

Apparently, he has learned that he can use her addiction to get what he wants. He can mistreat her thoroughly, and she'll endure it because she just can't say no to him.

In all these cases, we see how a person-addiction *de*values the addict while *over*valuing the object of the addiction. "He's not worth it!" friends say. "You deserve better!" But the addict's vision is warped; she can't see that.

And it's not just the addict who's hurt. The object of the addiction can get a bit warped, too. Laurie's boss is confirmed in his desire for a winner-take-all relationship. He knows nothing of the joy of give-and-take.

I once dined with a woman who exhibited traits of person-addiction, though at the time she had not latched on to anyone in particular. She was constantly filling my water glass, offering me food, warming my coffee, attending to my every need (while ignoring my wife, who was also there). It was downright uncomfortable to be worshiped in that way, but that was how she had learned to treat men. She was a servant, meeting the needs of the master.

Frankly, I worry about her as she develops new relationships. With her attitude, I don't know how her new relationships can be healthy. I suspect that some good men will be chased away by her overattention. The ones she'll attract will be selfish couch potatoes who want a waitress more than a wife.

But that's what addiction does. It tilts the playing field so that all participants are at a disadvantage.

Person-addiction also occurs in nonromantic relationships. Same-sex friendships (especially among women) can foster emotional dependencies. In these cases, a person's entire life—emotional state, self-confidence, energy—can hinge on a friend's presence or support.

Families see their share of person-addiction. Parents often get hooked on a child. They live their lives through their offspring and refuse to let go. Consider the stage mother who pushes a daughter into performing or the father who pressures his son to excel at sports. Often it seems as if the parents are fulfilling their own dreams of stardom and identifying too much with their young ones. But that can happen in many subtler ways as well. A parent may become overinvolved emotionally with a teenager's love life or a young adult's job choices. Obviously, a certain amount of concern and guidance is necessary, but sometimes it crosses a point of rationality. Sometimes a child realizes, "This isn't about me or my choices anymore, is it? It's about you and what you wish you had done."

The same kind of idol worship that can occur in an addictive marriage or a dating relationship can occur in a family. A parent can idolize a child. A child can idolize an older sibling or a parent. I know several adults who are essentially controlled by their parents' opinions. They are convinced that they could never make a good choice on their own. They need the guidance of a perfect mom or a do-no-wrong dad. That, too, is a form of person-addiction.

A MIXED BAG

Even as we look at the people in our group, we note that some show symptoms of different types of addictions. That is not unusual. Love addiction, sex addiction, and person-addiction are related and sometimes hard to distinguish. Social scientists find that drug addicts, when cured, often gravitate toward another addiction, such as drinking, smoking, or gambling. So it is with relationship addictions. In our group, Karen seems to have begun with a person-addiction to her ex-husband. She came to accept her divorce but settled into what might be considered a love addiction, needing to be in a relationship, though moving quickly from man to man. Yet she has settled on one man again, and she shows signs of a new person-addiction as she endures his abuse.

These transitions are common; as people change, their needs change, and their relationships change. I counseled Joan, who progressed through several types of relationship addictions. After Joan went through a divorce, she felt a significant void in her life. Even though she knew she wasn't ready for a relationship, she fantasized about men she met. They were usually romantic fantasies in which she was swept off her feet by the object of her attention and delivered from the pain of a meaningless life. She soon became obsessed with actually going out with these men, and she acted quite seductively in their presence. She frightened several potential dates away, but she finally landed one of her conquests and began to date him on a regular basis.

Joan felt an intense need to be with him every day; therefore, the relationship progressed very quickly. He soon became the sole object of her obsession, which fed into his desire for an intense sexual relationship. Although she was uneasy with his excessive demands, she was afraid she might lose his love, and so she gave in. He grew more and more demanding, even abusive, and Joan fell deeper and deeper into a pit of despair—feeling no comfort in the relationship and yet feeling too dependent to give him up.

Over a period of months, the relationship burned itself out. His sex addiction made him grow tired of her and move on. Otherwise, Joan confesses, "I would not have had the courage to end the relationship." In the aftermath, she felt used, discarded, cheap, and even more emotionally empty than before.

But Joan's despair led her to pursue a new love—one that would be different—somehow more fulfilling this time. If only she could find the right man . . .

And so the addictive cycle continues.

Chapter Three

CASE STUDY: SALLY

Sally came to my office as an addictive romance was winding down. Her man was pulling away from her. His calls were less frequent. Alone on weekends, she drank. Her life was falling apart.

When did the trouble start? You might trace it to her upbringing. Sally's mother seemed overly concerned about leaving her alone with her father. Sally never hugged him or had a loving relationship with him.

Or you might trace the trouble to her marriage. In gleeful rebellion against her parents, she married a man fourteen years her senior. She was just happy that someone that much older, and so much more educated, would take an interest in her. He became her father figure, controlling her life. Over their twenty-three years of marriage, he subtly chipped away at her self-esteem. She had to rely on him for everything. When someone asked her a question, she'd look to him for the answer.

And he hit her when he thought it was necessary.

Leave him? How could she do that? She had children to raise. She had no education. By herself, she was worth nothing—or such was the notion he had drummed into her. She began to take pills to ease the pain.

Or the trouble might have begun when she got a part-time job. The kids were in school, and the family needed the money. Then it became a full-time job. Then she started to earn her college degree, one course at a time. She was becoming her own person—and he didn't like it. The marriage used to be about meeting his needs. Now she had needs of her own, and he felt threatened.

The result was turmoil in the family. In a fierce attempt to regain control of his family, he "disowned" their teenage daughter for a trivial offense. After taking every pill in the medicine cabinet, Sally ended up in the intensive care unit. Her psychiatrist urged that the husband leave home.

He did. But there was more trouble ahead.

A LAW TO HIMSELF

On the day her husband walked out, Sally went to a lawyer friend, Jerry. He would not handle her divorce, but he recommended a female lawyer across the street. Sally walked to that office, filed the papers, returned to Jerry's office, and was asked out to dinner. The "dinner" lasted all evening. Sally had another powerful man in her life.

He was a bit older, obviously well educated, and out of her league. Thrice-divorced, he was his own man, living the good life. He could wine and dine women in style. Sally dreamed that maybe he would finally settle down with her, but she was aware that he was dating other women, too.

"It was a relationship very much like my marriage," she says now, looking back. "I had him up on a pedestal. He was a lawyer. I was still a mere person. Why would he be interested in me? He treated me really nice. I was impressed. We went sailing often on his boat, but never once did we get together with his friends. He was ashamed of me." She became controlled by his opinion of her. She bought clothes that she thought he would approve of.

She tried to act in a way he would like. She was not herself with him. She wasn't sure anymore who "herself" was.

From the first night, the relationship was physical. That met a deep need within Sally, her childhood lack of loving touch, but she felt used by Jerry. He would drop her off early from dates, complaining that he didn't feel well, and then (she'd learn later) he went off to see another woman. Sally loved the times she spent with him, but she resented all the times without him. He stopped calling as often, and she began drinking more and more alcohol.

That's when she came to see me. She described her desperation, the ache of being by herself, her drunken binges each weekend. For a few more months she continued in a painful cycle. She would determine to stop seeing him, to stop giving in to him sexually. But then he'd call, and she'd lose her resolve. "I'd hear his voice," she says now, "and I'd forget all the meanness. He would say one word, and all I had decided would go out the window." Once again, she was in a man's power.

Then he was gone for good, and her withdrawal was severe. She recalls, "I wasn't happy with myself, without someone else there. I had to have a relationship." She had no friends at the time. Most people she knew from her marriage had abandoned her, and she had made no new friends while with Jerry. She knew a few coworkers casually but not well enough to get much help. The drinking got even worse. She was suicidal. I was afraid for her.

THE SALESMAN

Richard was a salesman who called on the store where Sally worked. They struck up a friendship. About six months after the previous relationship had fizzled, Richard started asking Sally out. She jumped at the opportunity. He was, rather literally, a lifesaver—a caring, attentive man. A few months later, she learned that he was married.

Still, Richard bolstered her self-esteem, at least for a while. She notes, "He was telling me all along how good I was for him.

I did everything right. I did everything better than his wife did. I cooked better, I cleaned better, and I kept my car cleaner than she did. I was really soaking this all up. I treated my kids better than she treated hers. I cleaned the cat's litter box better than she did. Can you imagine? Yeah, but he was married to her."

That meant Sally's weekends were still lonely. She managed to rendezvous with Richard as he traveled his sales circuit in towns eighty to one hundred miles away. At that distance they could dine out and spend the evening in a motel. Sally would drive out to meet him once or twice a week, flushed with excitement over their tryst. She would drive home the next morning feeling awful.

Once again, the relationship was physical. Sally longed to be held, to be loved, and it felt good in Richard's arms. The good feelings would last through the night. Reality hit when the alarm went off.

"I felt like scum," she says. "It had become very demeaning." For two years she followed the pattern. Her life was all about taking drugs and drinking and driving the turnpike. She would be drinking *while* driving the turnpike. It was the only way she felt she could get through it all. She knew the relationship had no future, but she could not say no to it. She states, "Yet as much pain as it was, the feeling I had for those several hours was almost worth it."

In some ways, Richard was good for Sally. He was not a user, at least not as much as Sally's other men had been. He took an interest in her family, and he willingly became a part of her life— even though he had to exclude Sally from his family life. Sally's kids liked him; they did things together. But they never knew he was married.

Sally dreamed that someday she and Richard would be together for good. She knew that was unlikely, and he made no promises, but she kept dreaming. "I believe he really cared for me," she says now. "But he had a fine life with his wife and children. He wasn't going to leave them." And so she played that mental game of Ping-Pong, bouncing between hope and despair.

Richard took a vacation with his wife, and when he returned, things were different. He was easing out of Sally's life. That sent her into more bouts of drinking and taking prescription drugs. She had stopped seeing me by then, but she knew she needed help. She was absent from work more than she was present. Her kids would call in and say she was sick when really she was smashed out of her mind.

GETTING HELP

Sally admits, "I got tired of being sick, tired of drinking. A friend at work had mentioned that there was an evening rehab program in the area. I figured I could go there and still carry on my normal life. When I asked my friend about it, she said, 'No, you need detox.'" So Sally made arrangements to go to a local institution for three days to dry out. With a blood-alcohol level of .40, she could hardly see straight on the drive there. She stayed five weeks. When medical problems arose, she was transferred to a hospital. "I'm lucky I'm alive," she says. "They told me in the detox unit that I almost died."

After leaving the hospital, she got involved with Alcoholics Anonymous. She attends AA meetings regularly, and she speaks very highly of the program. It has contributed greatly to her healing.

As she sits here and tells her story, she's been clean and sober for one year, one month, and nine days. The drying-out process has also given her strength to confront her tendencies toward addictive relationships. She has a new self-esteem she never had before.

"Boy, do I like myself!" she says. "I don't have a romantic relationship with anybody right now, but I've made a lot of friends in the program. And I've learned I can do things on my own. I'm not afraid to be alone. It's really a neat feeling. I feel worthwhile. I'm not looking for a romance now. If it comes along, I'll consider it, but I'm not looking for it. I'm okay by myself."

Recently, Sally had some legal business, and she had to see

Jerry, her old lover/lawyer. She reports that she did so without a pang of regret. He had held power over her—his voice would melt all her resolve. She had allowed him to use her in the past, but she no longer had feelings for him—not even anger. They went about their business and she left. No longing looks. No heartfelt sighs. Nothing.

What's the difference between then and now? "I'm much more sure of myself," she explains. "I have my self-esteem back. I am important. I count." It's good to hear her say that.

EVALUATION

What type of relationship addiction did Sally have? I'd say she had them all, with substance addictions thrown in. She seems to have love hunger from her childhood. Her father's distance, her mother's suspicious nature, and later her husband's abuse combined to create a very needy woman.

These needs came out physically in her sexual relations with the various men in her life. She complained that her husband would touch her only when *he* wanted to, that he cared little for her sexual needs. Although her later affairs were more passionate, the same pattern seemed to be in place. She wanted love and offered sex. She was used and disappointed. Hers is a common pattern for female sex addicts.

However, she longed for more than sex. It was a stepping-stone to a deeper relationship—or so she hoped. Her low self-esteem made her "need" to be with somebody. The affair with the lawyer was both exhilarating and defeating. His status lifted her up for a time but then dashed her to the ground when she realized he would never marry her. She gave up all her personal boundaries with both Jerry and Richard. Even though Richard showed genuine love for her, they met on his terms, and she demeaned herself with those long inebriated drives. "I'm nobody unless somebody loves me" quickly turned into "I'll do whatever I have to do to win and keep someone's love." That was the downward spiral of the love addict, seeking to be somebody by being with somebody.

Sally showed signs of person-addiction as well. Her lengthy stay in an abusive marriage was the first example. She says her husband "chipped away" at her self-esteem to the point that she had no opinions of her own. Her husband was her god. When she finally broke free from him, with a few early stabs at self-awareness, she quickly chose a new god to worship. Jerry was "out of her league," and she was just tickled that somebody like him would pay attention to her. She willingly closed her eyes to his philandering and dreamed of an eventual paradise with him. Her relationship with Richard was just a fantasy. After all, that's what an extramarital affair is. There is none of the commitment and hard work required in a truly loving relationship. Still, she viewed him as a savior of sorts. He helped her when she needed it—and so she conveniently forgot that he was an unfaithful husband. Her willful ignorance of the flaws of her lover was a hallmark of person-addiction.

Sometimes a person has to hit bottom before healing can start. That seemed to be Sally's case. Ironically, the crisis of her chemical dependency probably forced her to look at the self-esteem issues that spawned her relationship addictions. That dependency also nearly killed her.

But she went back to square one. She took a hard look at her basic assumptions about herself. And for now, she's looking and sounding good. She knows that relapse is possible. She knows there are dangerous times ahead. But she is arming herself with the awareness of her needs and an appreciation of her value. That will help her get out of the dark woods.

Chapter Four

CHARACTERISTICS OF ADDICTIVE RELATIONSHIPS

J ust when is someone addicted?
Is a wife who stays in a difficult marriage in an addictive relationship, or is she demonstrating committed sacrificial love?

What about a single woman who prefers to go out with a man she is not too thrilled about rather than stay home on a Saturday night?

Or what about the man who has had twelve relationships in the past five years? Is he an addict, or is he just a man who likes to date?

And how about the woman who calls her mother every day, sometimes two or three times a day, and tells her every detail of her life—often before she tells her husband? Is this woman addicted to the maternal relationship, or is she just a good daughter?

These distinctions can be elusive without a look at the characteristics of addictive relationships. If we define *addiction* as "the drive to be with and *stay* with a particular person," most committed relationships have some element of addiction. Likewise, some element of true love is associated with most addictive relationships when *love* is defined as "the desire to commit and sacrifice your good for the good of another."

So we seem to have a continuum between lovingly healthy relationships and severely addictive ones. Most romances and good friendships fall somewhere between the two. So what's the difference? Where is the danger point on that scale? Where do Romeo and Juliet turn into . . . well, Romeo and Juliet? (That is, when does tender love become suicidal angst?)

CHARACTERISTICS OF AN ADDICTIVE RELATIONSHIP

There may be no specific dividing line on that continuum between healthy and unhealthy relationships. But as we observe relationships on both ends, we can come up with a number of basic differences between them. Then as we get a picture of healthy and unhealthy relationships, we can better evaluate the health of relationships. You don't need to sound the alarm if you recognize only one or two of these "symptoms" from your relationships, but if the overall pattern looks familiar, it's a good thing you're reading this book.

1. Free choice vs. compulsion

In a truly loving relationship, the partners freely choose to be with each other, to be associated with each other, to love each other. In an unhealthy addictive relationship, the free choice is replaced by compulsion. You simply *have* to be with that person, whether you really want to or not, observes Howard Halpern in *How to Break Your Addiction to a Person*.

Compare this situation to that of the cocaine addict. The drug inhibits the freedom to choose by controlling the user's mind and emotions. In a way, the addict makes a free choice with every snort, but the drug itself biologically stacks the deck in favor of drug use. The more the addict chooses the drug, the more it controls him, and the less freedom he enjoys.

So it is with the addictive relationship. The biology is slightly different, but the principle remains. Your brain gets used to certain impulses from the relationship. In a way, they drive a rut into the pathways of your mind. You may think you are making choices, but the more involved you get in the relationship, the more it controls your life. You feel powerless to break it off, and therefore, your freedom of choice is limited. The deeper the relationship becomes, the more control it has over your life.

In the healthy relationship, you are still drawn to the person and willing to sacrifice to make it work, but you maintain objectivity. Your judgment overrides your emotions, which helps you remain in control of your choices. That means you hold the other person accountable for her actions. You will not stand for mistreatment, and you will recognize when your love goes unreciprocated.

Becky and Bob dated for a while and grew together very quickly. As their relationship progressed, Becky noticed Bob taking her more and more for granted. He called at the last minute or just stopped by and then hung around watching television. He made himself at home with her; he ate her food and took advantage of her generous nature. He also made it clear that he expected a sexual relationship on his terms. When she complained that they never went out anymore, he usually commented on his need to save money, and he promised a special date on an unspecified occasion.

Despite Bob's treatment, Becky was so emotionally drawn to him that she dared not risk making him mad. With little complaint, she continued to feed and wait on him whenever he came over. But Becky found that the more she gave, the more empty she felt inside, especially after she had given in to him sexually. To numb the uneasy feeling, she tried harder and harder to show him how much she loved him, hoping that he would try harder to love her. But in reality, other than a few times when she saw glimmers of hope, the relationship only worsened.

Becky felt utterly frustrated with the relationship, and her friends began to question what she saw in Bob, so she decided to try to break it off. Yet whenever she tried to rehearse how she would do it, she convinced herself that "now is not a good time," or "if I wait a bit longer, perhaps he'll change." Over a period of months, instead of breaking off with Bob, Becky grew even more emotionally dependent. She detached from many of her friends because she had less and less time for them and because she tired of hearing their negative opinions about Bob.

The relationship finally ended about a year later when Bob began seeing someone else. Becky was devastated. Adding to her depression over the loss of the relationship was her loss of contact with almost all of her former friends. She felt emotionally and spiritually isolated.

Why had Becky stayed with Bob so long? Was she in love with him? Had she maintained her objectivity? Or was she driven by an empty feeling inside that limited her ability to choose to pursue (or not pursue) the relationship?

You may be thinking, *What Becky put up with was nothing in comparison to what I've gone through.* Indeed, there are far more severe stories to tell. For many, the compulsion to stay in the relationship at any cost has led to the toleration of physical, sexual, and emotional abuse. As we sink deeper and deeper into the relationship, the power of the compulsive drive seems to deepen. We end up compromising most of our standards, beliefs, and values just to maintain the very thing in life that is hurting us the most.

2. Mutual support vs. attempt to rescue

Have you ever known people who always seemed to date "beneath" themselves? The sweet, innocent girl who dates the drug addict? The upstanding young man who goes out with the emotional wreck? Certainly, we shouldn't overgeneralize these cases, and that whole concept of someone being "beneath" someone else in value is a dangerous one. But these situations are often unhealthy because they are unbalanced from the start. The motivation underlying such relationships is often not love at all but pity, pride, or a compulsive need to save someone.

In healthy relationships, both partners help each other to

function, to grow, to "be all each can be." In addictive relationships, one person tries to rescue, fix, reform, save, or at least enable the other. There is a constant tilt to the relationship. One is always in need; the other needs to be needed. They become dependent on each other in this lopsided state, which we call codependency.

I knew a woman in college who was a classic codependent. She was a Christian, strong in her faith, but she always gravitated toward the guys with shady backgrounds. I found the tendency especially frustrating because I was attracted to her. But she would never go out with me because I wasn't needy enough. She was into what I called missionary relationships. I watched as she took a friend of mine under her wing. He had become a Christian in prison, serving time for armed robbery and drug possession. He was a brand-new Christian, trying to grow in his faith. She was ready to help him in personal Bible study and spiritual development. But the Bible study, as you might guess, developed into something a little more personal. Soon they were romantically involved.

I don't know what happened to that relationship. Perhaps it lasted. Perhaps he grew in his faith with her help, and maybe they learned to treat each other as partners. But I doubt it.

You see, that's the problem with codependency. It is built on one's need and the other's need-meeting. What happens when the new Christian grows into spiritual maturity? What does the "missionary" do then? The whole basis of the relationship has shifted. She is not needed anymore, at least not in the same way.

Ray told me of his dating relationship with a woman who had recently been divorced. When he met her, she was still devastated by her husband's desertion. Ray was able to bring her some joy and to rebuild her confidence.

Though she was determined not to rush into a rebound relationship, she was emotionally needy, and Ray was ready to meet her needs. He thrived on the need-meeting. The friendship moved quickly into a romance. Ray figured, "It was important for her to feel desirable again." He loved the fact that he was restoring her to wholeness.

A funny thing happened. She became whole again. She didn't need him anymore. The tilted ground on which their romance rested had become level, and that changed everything. Fortunately, they both realized it and broke up rather amicably.

Ray added an interesting footnote. Within a year after their breakup, the woman married a man who had been through a painful divorce. She had found someone with whom she could engage in mutual support.

And Ray's next relationship? A struggling single mother.

Codependents need dependents. The examples here have been rather mild. We could find many cases of alcoholics or drug abusers and their codependent spouses. The codependent gets hooked on helping the dependent.

The problem is that the whole relationship is built on crisis. The rescuer is actually in a catch-22. Rescuing the dependent, restoring the needy person to health, will shake the relationship. The rescuer can't get high on helping anymore if the dependent doesn't need more help. So, subconsciously, the rescuer has a vested interest in keeping the dependent dependent. The codependent enters into the addictive cycle.

3. Objectivity vs. rose-colored glasses

In a healthy relationship, each partner recognizes the value and the shortcomings of the other. In an addictive relationship, one partner denies any negative aspects of the other. "He's perfect," a woman might say, "the man of my dreams." The onlooker might see a million things wrong with him and how he treats her, but the woman in love is blind to all that.

"Love is blind." So goes the old adage. But if first love is to grow into anything healthy over the long term, it had better open its eyes.

I'm not trashing the idea of maintaining a positive mental attitude. It's good to look for the positive aspects of the people we meet. But we need to be objective. It is naive and dangerous to ignore the negative.

Such rose-colored glasses are common when people are infatuated. You may know this feeling: "You're wonderful. You're the answer to all my problems. You're exactly what I've been looking for all my life." This natural phase usually occurs at the start of a relationship.

In *The Road Less Traveled*, M. Scott Peck describes the "myth of romantic love" in this way: "We have met the person for whom all the heavens intended us, and since the match is perfect, we will then be able to satisfy all of each other's needs forever and ever."

We willingly put aside the problems that arise. We are in love: "I only have eyes for you." As I said, this natural feeling occurs in many lives. For a time, it's healthy and fun. In fact, without such temporary blindness, men and women might never get together.

Peck wryly adds that the myth of romantic love, though a "dreadful lie," may be "a necessary lie, in that it ensures the survival of the species by its encouragement and seeming validation of the falling-in-love experience that traps us into marriage."

We find an affirmation of such infatuation even in the Bible, in the lyrical Song of Solomon. The woman in love sings, "Like an apple tree among the trees of the woods, so is my beloved among the sons" (2:3). In other words, you are the best I could possibly find. This is love-talk, the language of infatuation.

The problem occurs when infatuation refuses to grow up. Falling in love is a natural phase, and so is the fading of those feelings. Healthy relationships grow into an objective, responsible love that weathers the storms of life. As love matures, each partner begins to see the other's bad side—and everyone has one.

Similarly, the infatuated person feels omnipotent. She is walking on air. Let the world rush past. Maybe millions of people go by, but they all disappear from view 'cause I only have eyes for you. You and me against the world. I got you, babe—and nothing else matters.

But growth means opening one's eyes to the rest of the world. Growth means reestablishing a certain distance from the other person. Growth means understanding the limits of the person and the borders of the relationship. If that growth does not occur, the relationship is stunted. It can remain in that infantile state for many years.

I knew a couple in my church who seemed to stay in the infatuation stage too long. Even after a year of dating, they seemed very much "in love." They couldn't keep their hands off each other. Every time I saw them they were all googly-eyed, gazing into each other's eyes.

I was surprised that they were still at that point after being together a year. I talked with them soon after they were engaged, and I asked them about positive *and negative* characteristics of each other. The answers I got were all positive: "I couldn't live without her"; "When he's away from me, I feel empty inside, and when he's near, I'm complete."

Sounds wonderful, right? In fact, I'm glad my wife wasn't with me at the time. She might say, "Why don't you ever talk about me like that? Why don't you love me in that way?"

But that misses the point of what true love is. Love doesn't mean that I can't live without you or you're all I could ever dream of. Love means that I recognize your good points and bad points, I entrust you with mine, and I still commit myself to be true to you, to serve and be served, to honor and be honored.

Too many couples panic when the infatuation fades. They say, "We're falling out of love!" But the fact is, that's just when true love begins to grow. In unhealthy relationships, people reach for the rose-colored glasses: "If I allow myself to see the bad side, that will destroy the feelings that make me feel so good." In healthy relationships, people risk honesty—both in sharing and in seeing—to grow into a more mature love.

Mature love also means that the partners hold each other accountable for actions. If, say, your partner doesn't show up for an important date, what are you going to do? You could make excuses for your partner. You could accept your partner's flimsy excuses without a word of protest. That's the rose-colored glasses method.

But a healthy love would confront the situation in a firm but forgiving way: "That date was very important to me. It hurt me a lot that you didn't show up. But besides my pain, I'm concerned about our relationship. It makes me think that you don't care about 'us.' If your excuse is true, I forgive you, but you can't keep standing me up like that. That's not the kind of relationship that's good for either of us."

By stepping back and viewing things objectively, you can make wise decisions about what's good for you, your partner, and the relationship.

4. Balance with other friends vs. exclusive attention

What happened to Ricki? She used to be so active in our singles group. She had many friends of both sexes who supported her and received support from her as we all went through the various crises of singleness. We cheered her on as she told us of a promising new relationship in her life. Tony was attentive, sensitive to her needs; he showered her with flowers and took her to places she loved. She had dated more than her share of skunks, and we were glad for her good fortune.

Then we stopped seeing her. She begged out of our group activities. A few of us phoned her and were treated politely, but Ricki seemed distant. Sue managed to arrange a shopping trip with her, and she reported that Ricki was constantly worried about what Tony would think of this dress, that blouse, those stockings. The conversation revolved around Tony. Ricki, it seemed, had no other life.

That was six years ago. We all lost touch with her.

Then, recently, Ricki called Sue. They got together over coffee at a local diner, and Ricki unfolded her story.

She had married Tony. His constant attention had won her over; she felt extremely loved, desired, prized. She was his trophy.

But Tony was the jealous type, and soon she became a prisoner in her home. Yes, his jealousy made her sever ties with the singles group. Even while they were dating, he was suspicious of those friendships and pressured her to break them. Then when they married, the jealousy got even worse. He grilled her about any contact she had with anyone. She was even afraid to speak to the letter carrier.

She had a child, and she gained a great deal of weight. She felt undesirable, and Tony apparently thought so, too. The child was his prize, and Ricki was just a nurse. He went on long business trips and carried on affairs with little attempt to hide them, but he kept checking up on Ricki. He still discouraged any outside friendships.

There she was, locked in a bad marriage. She had cut herself off from the friends who could help her; she felt unworthy of new friendships; she had a baby to take care of. She told Sue about how Tony, in a drunken rage, had pulled out a gun and threatened her: "If you ever fool around on me . . ." That was when she knew she had to get out.

Sue gave her encouragement and practical advice, but there was a wall between them. Ricki had cut herself off from her closest friends, and it wasn't easy to restore those friendships. She did move out and divorce Tony, but she never came back to the church or renewed friendships among the singles group.

That's an extreme case, but its patterns are not unusual. You may know some people with similar stories. A jealous boyfriend or girlfriend. Severed friendships. An exclusive focus on that one relationship. Then, often, abuse of the relationship.

Exclusivity is not always so one-sided, not always the result of jealousy. Sometimes two people feel so passionately about each other that both want to spend all their time together. Their other friendships slip away. Suddenly, the guy you play basketball with on Thursday nights can't make it. He's out with his girlfriend. Suddenly, the girl in the theater group has to drop out of the cast because she's spending all her time with her new beau.

Like infatuation, this phase is natural. But when it goes on too long, it gets dangerous. The implication behind exclusive relationships is this: two people in love can meet all of each other's needs. That isn't true. That guy needs to play basketball—and her jump shot is lousy. She needs to act, but he doesn't know Tennessee Williams from Mississippi mud pie. To be whole, the two people need to do the things they love, and they need to maintain the friendships that have supported them. Yes, there will be some adjustments as the couple grow closer. Each schedule will shift a bit as they make time to be together. But neither partner needs to have complete dibs on the other. That's unwhole and unhealthy.

In a healthy relationship, both partners know that they have *priority* but not *exclusivity* in the other's life. Many needs are met within the relationship, but others are met outside it. Each partner can and should share friends with the other, but longtime friendships should not threaten a romantic relationship.

I have healthy and unhealthy examples from my life. As I was recovering from my divorce, I began to date someone who met a lot of my needs. And I was very needy. I latched on to her and began to take and take and take. She was a very nurturing person, so she was very happy to give and give and give. (It was one of those rescue relationships that can be therapeutic for a time but seldom lasts.)

We began to see each other every day. She would cook dinner for me regularly, but sometimes I had to work until 9:00 or 9:30 at night. Even then, I'd get home and call her immediately. She would say, "Why don't you come over, even for a few minutes? I haven't seen you all day. I miss you. I'd like to be with you." Of course, I felt the same way.

So we began to spend all our time together. I didn't go fishing with the guys anymore because I wanted to be with her (and she wasn't interested in fishing). My other activities and friendships were preempted because I was "in love" with the woman.

As you might guess, the relationship didn't last. As I grew back to emotional health, I didn't need her as much. And I became aware that our whole relationship was based on *my* need. We broke up with considerable pain for both of us.

A few years later I began another relationship. By that time I had gained a number of new friends, I was involved heavily in my church, and I'd begun to work in Fresh Start, a divorce recovery program. I was very interested in the new woman, but she was busy, too. We could see each other only every two or three weeks.

As our relationship grew, we spent more and more time together, but neither of us scrapped old friendships. We recognized that those friendships and activities were part of who we were and part of what we brought to each other. Each allowed the other to spend that necessary time with friends.

That woman is now my wife. And to this day, we maintain separate friendships. She goes out with "the girls" sometimes; I go out with "the boys." We meet many of each other's needs, but there are other social and recreational needs we can't meet for each other. We don't have to.

5. Trust vs. jealousy

"Where were you?"

"Who were you with?"

"I saw the way you looked at her! What's going on?"

"Why can't we be together more often? Is there someone else?"

Jealousy is an ugly monster. It can take over a relationship and destroy it. Jealousy is born of insecurity and desire. It is not known to be reasonable. Wild charges are made, exposing deep feelings of pain or fear. If you have been jealous within a relationship, you know how it gnaws at you, defying your attempts to control it. If your partner has been the jealous one, you know how frustrating it can be to sidestep the traps that monster sets.

The jealous person fears that the partner will leave for someone more physically attractive, more interesting, more suitable, or more financially stable. This possibility creates panic and results in irrational attempts to control the partner's life. This reaction can chase the partner away unless the partner is addicted, too.

Underlying the jealousy is the convoluted logic of relationship addiction: "I am not worth anything. By myself, I am miserable. But with this other person by my side, I am worth something; I am happy. I need this person. But since I am not worth anything, my partner is bound to find someone else who is worth more. That person will steal my partner away, and I will be miserable again. So I need to prepare for that or guard against that and keep my partner from finding anyone else." In the process, everyone becomes miserable. Jealous people fulfill their prophecy in a way. Convinced of their unworthiness, they sabotage whatever happiness is within their grasp.

I knew a woman who was overcome by jealousy about her boyfriend. Let's call her Ann. Every day she would call Brian and ask about his day. (That's nice; there's nothing wrong so far.) She'd say, "So, what did you do today?"

The broad question would usually bring a vague answer: "Oh, nothing much. I went to work, worked on some projects, went home." (Anything objectionable there? No, but Ann has to keep digging for something.)

"Did you talk to anybody today?"

"Sure," Brian would answer. "We had some meetings, and a bunch of us went to lunch." *(A bunch of us? What is he hiding?* she thinks.*)*

"Oh," Ann would say gently. "Who all did you talk to at work or at lunch?"

"No one special. Joe and Pete in my office. And Mr. Williams stopped in about that project." (Nothing yet.)

"Well, who was at lunch?"

"Oh, the guys. You know. Barry from the mailroom and Carl and Art and Sally." (Bingo!)

"Sally? Did you talk with her?"

"Yeah, a little."

"About what?"

Brian would pause as he tried to remember the trivial conversation of earlier that day—or, as she interpreted it, to come up with a good story. "I don't know. About the job mostly."

"What did you say about the job?"

By then, Brian would be a bit peeved. "I don't know, Ann. It was a silly conversation over lunch, okay? I don't remember what we said. It wasn't important." (Right.)

"Well, you don't have to get upset. I'm just interested in your life. If you don't want me to be interested . . ." *(I must be on to something,* Ann figures. *He's getting defensive.)*

"No, Ann, I'm glad you're interested in my life. I'm interested in yours, too."

"So, Brian, do you have lunch with Sally very often?"

"No! Well, yes, but no. It's not that. It's just a bunch of us. We work together. Sally's one of the group." (Brian has stepped into the quicksand.)

"But you talk with her. Do you like talking with Sally?"

"No!"

"So she forces herself on you."

"No, it's not like that! I talk to everyone. Sally happened to sit across from me." (Oops! A detail better left unsaid.)

"And do you think that was an accident?"

"What?"

"That Sally sat across from you. I'm a woman. I know these things. She's after you, Brian, and I don't like it. I don't think you ought to talk to Sally anymore."

"But, Ann—"

"Promise me you won't talk to Sally."

"But I work with—"

"Who's more important to you . . . Sally or me?"

"You, of course, but—"

"Well, I'm not so sure about that. You seem to be standing up for her. Was she the one working late with you last Thursday when you were late to dinner?"

"There was a bunch of us."

"I've heard that before . . ."

And suddenly, all the old laundry gets taken out and spread across the relationship. Ann has turned a friendly chat into the Spanish Inquisition. She has decided that this working colleague is the Other Woman. She has assumed that a casual lunch with coworkers amounted to a private romantic tryst.

I changed a few of the details, but this conversation is typical of the ones Ann and Brian told me about in counseling. They would have huge fights over minor items, then they'd get back together, and the jealous rage would build again.

Obviously, it was not a healthy relationship. They had to learn to trust each other. Ann, especially, had to learn to trust Brian. But more than that, she had to trust that she was good enough for Brian. Her need to control Brian's life came out of a lack of appreciation for her life.

The fact is, Brian could have been dating Sally. Ann's irrational suspicions may have been right. The problem was that the very thought threw Ann into a panic. How would she live without him? If she was convinced that she *could* live quite well without him, there would be no such panic. She could still express her love for Brian and her desire for a committed relationship, but she would not react with desperation to the possibility that he might choose otherwise. Her life would go on, regardless.

In some cases, the addicted person is the *object* of the partner's jealousy. That was the case with Ricki. She should have seen signs of dangerous possessiveness in Tony, but she was blind to it. Her lack of self-appreciation made her crave the appreciation he was showing, even if that made her a trophy and dehumanized her.

The dual nature of Christ's command, "Love your neighbor *as yourself,*" comes into play here. The antidote for jealousy is to "trust your partner *as you trust yourself.*" Your partner may disappoint you, may hurt you, or may run off with a coworker, but you need to trust yourself to be okay by yourself. That will help you avoid relationships with people who don't deserve trust (like Tony), and that will pave the way for open, trusting communication.

6. Recovery vs. continuing dysfunctions

Chapter 7 will deal with root causes of addictive relationships, but we also need to include this subject among the characteristics of such relationships. People who get into addictive relationships tend to come out of dysfunctional family patterns.

I don't want to be accused of using too much psychospeak, so let me offer a simple explanation. A dysfunction means that something doesn't work as it should. In fact, dysfunctions are usually patterns that go *against* the proper working of a person or a family.

When I'm driving my car, I have a problem if I have a flat tire. I might even consider it a crisis. And I could probably call it a *mis*function. The tire, being flat, isn't doing what a tire should. I stop and fix it and drive on.

But if my car is badly out of alignment, that's another thing. It affects my steering, the car wobbles to the right as I drive, and my tires get worn quickly on one side, leading to more flat tires. It might be considered a *dys*function. It's not just when one thing goes wrong. It's when the whole system goes out of whack.

So it is with families. In time, family crises can be dealt with and recovered from. But dysfunctions last. The family system is supposed to work a certain way. Love, nurture, discipline, education, and so on—these are the family's systems. If the parents are divorced, and the children see their father only once a month, that threatens to mess up the family systems. If the parents always fight or if they never talk to each other, they model unhealthy behaviors for their children. The family isn't working as it should. If one parent is an alcoholic, and the children are forced to go through the cycles of addiction, that will also create basic problems in the way the family works. Obviously, if there is spouse abuse or child abuse, sexual or otherwise, that will create long-term problems in the children's lives.

A person who fails to make a concerted effort to recover from those family dysfunctions is liable to repeat those errors in future relationships. When the Bible talks about children being punished for the "iniquity of the fathers" to the "third and the fourth generation" (Exod. 34:7), it has a grasp on some very modern data. Family dysfunctions are repeated and repeated and repeated. Messed-up children become messed-up parents. And the cycle continues.

From our group, Dawn and Ginnie illustrate this point. Dawn grew up with an alcoholic father, and she fought all her life for his affection. She's still fighting for it, only now she seeks it from other men. She jumps at the promise of affection from the men she dates, and she tends to scare them away with her zeal.

Ginnie's case is even more severe. Sexually abused by her father, she learned to equate sex with love. That was the only attention her father ever gave her. So now she, too, seeks fatherly affection, but she seeks it through sex—and is consistently disappointed.

There is healing. People can recover from a dysfunctional past, but it takes some hard work and a lot of help. Dawn and Ginnie are like countless others who seek counseling to dig up their past and lay it to rest again. But it doesn't happen overnight.

In addictive relationships, people tend to come from dysfunctional backgrounds—and tend not to deal with them. They continue to deny their deep-seated need even as it affects every choice they make. In healthy relationships, people have worked through that stuff or are diligently working through it.

7. Healthy independence vs. overdependence

People who get into addictive relationships tend to be emotionally dependent people. That is, they have a great inner drive to be connected with someone.

We all need other people; that's normal. But overdependent people feel they need people in their lives *all the time*. Or they want to have a special relationship with a particular person *all the time*. When they are by themselves, they feel lonely and empty. This feeling creates a certain desperation to be with someone— anyone! And that leads to poor relationship choices. When they do find someone to hook up with, their desperation tends to overburden the relationship. They demand too much.

The people in our group exhibited a lot of overdependence. "He's . . . like . . . inside of me. I need him," said Dawn. "I needed the guy more than he needed me," explained Margie. "I want to be with him all the time," Laurie added. That's the language of overdependence.

Each woman would be better off if she could learn to embrace healthy independence: "I'm fine on my own. If you want me, come and get me. I'm going to the movies Saturday; if you like, you can join me." That attitude would revolutionize those relationships.

8. A growing relationship vs. a love-hate cycle

"He's a really sexy guy," said Laurie, "but he's a real jerk, too." That kind of good news–bad news joke is common to addictive relationships. You love him, you hate him, but you can't get away from him; you need him.

A friend in college went through that regularly, and she took everyone else on the roller coaster with her. Cristy would get incredibly mad at her boyfriend, Will. For two days she would bad-mouth him to all her friends: "I don't know why I ever went out with him! He is so wrong for me! He has no compassion, no sensitivity! I don't care if I ever see him again!"

Then she'd see him again.

For the next few days, she'd coo and smile. Will was so wonderful. Will was perfect. Will was, once again, the man of Cristy's dreams.

Until they had another fight. Then he became a nightmare again.

Some people seem to thrive on such volatile relationships. But the crucial question is, Where is the relationship going? Are the two people growing together with each new disagreement? Or are they just replaying the same old issues? How do the partners handle conflict? Are they resolving it through healthy give-and-take? Or are they at an impasse, with neither giving in? When they do get back together, is it because they've decided to make the necessary compromises to work out their problem? Or do they just "need" each other so much that they decide to ignore the problem until it flares up again?

Every relationship has its disagreements. But in a healthy relationship, the partners talk through the problems, work through them, learn through them, learn about each other, learn about themselves, and move on. That's growth. That may mean the relationship reaches a higher level of understanding and commitment. Or that may mean the partners decide the romantic relationship isn't worth pursuing. Either way, the individuals grow as they deal with their conflicts.

Addictive relationships are characterized by unresolved conflicts. Any disagreement becomes a stumbling block. This goes along with the rose-colored glasses routine. You can't admit there might be a problem, so you sweep it under the rug. You keep sweeping it under the rug until one day it's so big you trip over it and fall flat on your face. Okay, maybe that metaphor got away from me, but the point is that conflicts need to be dealt with. Refusal to acknowledge them and resolve them just postpones the inevitable. Eventually, the conflict will blow up, and there will be a big fight. The love-hate cycle will continue.

Often such couples will make up and get back together. But too often they return on the same terms as before. Nothing is resolved. They have blown off steam by hating each other for a few days or weeks, and now they can sweep the problem under the rug again. (There's that rug again. Maybe it's being steam cleaned.) As long as the conflict goes unresolved, the partners are headed for another fight over the same old issues.

Healthy relationships are mountains to climb. There are rocks and cliffs and huge obstacles to surmount. Sometimes the climbers have to double back and try another route. It's not always easy, but they keep climbing.

Unhealthy relationships are whirlpools. The love-hate cycle goes around and around with no real advancement. And ultimately, the relationship goes down the drain.

9. Strengthening vs. weakening

Addicts feel invincible when they are using their drug. Euphoria reigns. They can do anything, meet any challenge, conquer the world—they feel great. The same is true of relationship addicts. When you are with that special person, things are good. When you are in the relationship you crave, you have a high. When you are engaging in the physical contact that gives you pleasure or having sex with the person you idolize, the world is yours.

But what about the morning after? What kind of hangover do you have? The sex addict wakes up in a strange bed and feels cheap. The love addict endures the insults or battering of an abusive partner. The person-addict sees all the flaws of that person and tries to ignore them once again.

The simple question is this: Does the relationship make you stronger? Healthy relationships do that. You wake up the next morning and feel better about yourself. You are empowered by that relationship to do what you need to do. Addictive relationships sap your strength. The temporary buzz yields to a lethargic life.

Did you hear that from the people in our group?

"Every day I think, *Okay this is the day it ends*. But then I see him, and I lose my nerve."

"I sat at home and moped."

"That's the way I am."

"For about six months now I've been trying to break up with him, but . . ."

Ironically, the one thing most of these people need to do, they don't have the strength for, and that is to end the relationship. That very relationship is sapping their strength. These are, for the most part, strong, successful women. Some of them thrive in the business world, making key decisions. Others run their households with skill and decisiveness. But these relationships reduce them to children. They think little of themselves. They are afraid of doing something wrong. They have no strength to control their lives.

And it's also ironic that the people who are strong enough to stand on their own, even to break off a close relationship, are those who don't need to. Healthy relationships give people the support needed to make key decisions, to feel confident, to communicate freely. And those are the relationships that ought to be held on to.

THE CYCLE

Addictive relationships follow certain patterns. Some people who go from relationship to relationship find themselves doing the same things in each one. Obviously, details may differ from person to person, but this is the general picture.

   1. Initial emptiness. You are in need. It may be the result of a recent disappointment—a breakup or divorce. Or it may be a general lack of self-esteem, perhaps a result of your upbringing.

   2. The connection. You meet a person who seems to offer what you need. Perhaps the person singles you out for attention, which pleases you. Or perhaps you decide to pursue someone.

3. Infatuation. The mind games begin. Infatuation is a normal start to many relationships, but you may go overboard this time. You begin to idolize the person. You think about the person often, remembering only good things, ignoring faults.

4. Feedback. At some point, friends may give you their opinions: "This relationship is bad for you." But what do they know?

5. Excuses. You make all kinds of excuses to yourself and to your friends. It's not as bad as they think—or so you say. You have nagging doubts about the relationship, but in many ways it's the best thing that's happened to you in a long time.

6. The turning. There is often a point where you commit to the relationship, just within yourself. You may distance yourself from your friends: "If you don't like him, then tough! I don't like you." At this stage, you tire of making excuses. You may scuttle your convictions about churchgoing, sexual morality, or what you'll put up with.

7. A step too far. The relationship may continue for a long time before something happens to jolt you back to your senses. Maybe your partner is unfaithful or abusive. Maybe you finally see how far you have plummeted. Whatever, there is new dissatisfaction with the relationship.

8. Panic. Whenever you think about ending the relationship, you get panicky, sometimes clinging to the person even more. After all, you have invested a great deal of yourself in this relationship. This double-mindedness— bouncing between steps 7 and 8—can continue for months or years.

9. Breakup. The relationship may never get to this point. But you may override the panic long enough to make a move to get free of the relationship. Or your partner may initiate the breakup, which causes great pain.

10. Withdrawal. After the breakup of an addictive relationship, you can expect to suffer withdrawal symptoms that are not only emotional but physical as well. Your body has grown used to the sensations of that relationship and now must readjust. In addiction, you've probably been through great tension in making the decision and/or suffered shock when the breakup finally occurred. Whatever, you feel lousy. What do you do?

11. Return to sender. Unfortunately, many people decide that the most obvious way to overcome their withdrawal symptoms is to go back into the relationship. They feel lousy, and that will make them feel better. Or so they figure. This is, in a sense, another turning, and they go back to step 6.

12. New game. The relationship is over for good, and you've fought through the withdrawal symptoms, but you still feel empty, alone, and lost. If you're smart, you'll restore contact with those friends you rejected around step 5 or 6. But too many go back to step 1. They feel empty, so they seek fulfillment in a new relationship. And the cycle starts all over again.

RECOGNIZING RELATIONSHIP ADDICTION

Now that we have covered some of the general characteristics of addictive relationships, the question is, Would you recognize them in *yourself* if they were there? Sometimes it is easier to see the weakness in others.

The following letter came to me recently. Read through it and see how many of the addictive characteristics you can spot. Then reread it and see if any of it sounds like you.

I am sitting here writing to you through tears, soliciting your prayers. I have been separated and divorced for two and a half years. I finally allowed myself to fall in love with a man with whom I've had a wonderful relationship for over five months now. We spent a lot of time together and became very close very quickly.

About two months ago, he told me he wanted to marry me. We knew that this was the direction we both wanted our relationship to go. Then, out of the blue, he announced that he couldn't go through with this and wants nothing to do with me. He insisted he meant everything he said about love and marriage, but he really needs to be single right now. When he told me this, he was very cold, detached, and somewhat hostile. He had never been this way before.

He told me he had a temper, but I had only seen it a couple of times, and I just figured he was having a tough time emotionally. He told me I was so good for him because I brought him closer to God. Before he met me, he told me, he was into porno films and occasionally went with prostitutes. Once he told me he would rape me unless I consented to have sex with him.

This may sound crazy to you. But I am an educated social worker and no dummy! I believed in this man, and I accepted his past as just that. It was in the *past!* He was a gentleman and treated me so well. We even prayed together and said grace before every meal. So I obviously believed him and trusted him.

Why then do my pastor, his pastor, and my therapist see this man as one with a character disorder and a sexual deviant? They tell me to get out of Dodge in a hurry and to count my blessings that he dumped me. None of them know him like I do.

I am emotionally devastated. I trusted, and now WHAM! Where did I go wrong? Now I'm grieving all over again, and this time it's worse than my marriage breakup. I don't know how I will go on without him.

I am probably the first one who ever loved him unconditionally. He even told me I was. Maybe he couldn't handle it. Who knows?

Please pray for me. My self-esteem is shot, and I feel so used. I still believe in my heart that he is a *good* man at his core. Pray that he will get help, too, before he goes out and does something stupid (i.e., rape).

Please send me anything you can that will help me. I have a lot of love to give to someone. Pray that I will find someone soon who can accept that love and who can share my same needs and desires.

My purpose is not to judge; it's to help. By shining the spotlight on this often-ignored subject of relationship addiction, perhaps some readers will be motivated to get the help they need. Perhaps some friends will sense what kind of help is needed.

The woman who sent this letter did a number of things right. She was praying. God's help is crucial to break an addiction, as any Twelve-Step program will tell you. She was seeking counsel from pastors, a therapist, and (through this letter) me. She said her self-esteem "is shot," but her letter points to a strong sense of self: "I finally allowed myself to fall in love"; "I am probably the first one who ever loved him unconditionally." Although she was confused and hurt, she was not curling up in self-pity and self-hate.

The letter, however, clearly depicts the dangers of codependency. She (a social worker) was trying to rescue the man. She felt that she was the only one who could get through to him. He needed her, and she thrived on being needed. (Note that her current frustration is that she has so much love to give, but no one needs it.) Although she was probably much more stable emotionally than he was, she became fixated on him. He became her reason for being. She was bringing him to health, to love, to God.

Also, did you see how many times she contradicted herself? Could you see her rose-colored glasses? She wrote, "[He was] a man with whom I've had a wonderful relationship," but "he told me he would rape me"; "He was a gentleman," but "pray that he will get help . . . before he . . . does something stupid."

Why did he break it off? We don't know. It may have been a flare-up of his sex addiction. Perhaps he didn't want to become healthy *just yet*. Perhaps she was smothering him with her zeal for rescuing. Reading between the lines, we might guess that he was not being totally honest with her about his addiction, his temper, his desires. Or perhaps she was refusing to accept the honest things he told her.

Relationship addiction is a powerful and dangerous thing. It grabs us at the core of who we are and makes us do things we'd never dream of. The drug addict would betray his own mother for a fix. The compulsive gambler would steal from her best friend to place "just one more bet." And the person addicted to love would sacrifice principles and friendships and self-respect to go out "just one more time" with that special person.

The first step in any safari is to identify the beast you're hunting. What does it look like? What are its habits? Where does it hang out? We've done this. We now know what addictive relationships look like.

But the next step is to gauge the level of danger. What kind of danger are you in? Are you in an addictive relationship or about to take the plunge? Or aren't you sure whether your current relationship should be considered addictive? Next chapter's test will answer some questions for you.

Chapter Five

TEST YOURSELF

You've read about three types of relationship addiction and nine of its major characteristics. Now it's time to evaluate yourself. Do you have a relationship addiction, either to a particular person or to a particular relationship? The following test will help you sort that out.

As you can see, your possible responses range in value from 1 (strongly disagree) to 7 (strongly agree). If you are totally unsure, don't skip the entry—just put a 4. Answer as honestly as possible how you feel about each sentence presented. And don't try to "psych out" the test. Don't try to figure out whether it's good or bad to answer a certain way. Some statements are really rather neutral. But taken together, your responses to them will provide helpful insight into your tendencies.

Lines are provided for your answers, but you may want to use a separate piece of paper. You may want to lend this book to a friend or retest yourself a year or two from now. (You may want to photocopy the scoresheet. It is important for analyzing your responses.)

RELATIONSHIP ADDICTION TEST

Key:

1—Strongly Disagree
2—Disagree Somewhat
3—Lean Toward Disagreeing
4—Neutral/Don't Know
5—Lean Toward Agreeing
6—Agree Somewhat
7—Strongly Agree

_____ 1. I do not feel happy unless I know that someone loves me.

_____ 2. I feel an irresistible impulse to pursue a person I am attracted to.

_____ 3. If I think someone really needs me, I am attracted to that person.

_____ 4. I do not have the resources within me to deal with the emotional pain I face.

_____ 5. When I am not in a steady loving relationship, I feel empty and needy.

_____ 6. I sometimes feel guilty about going too far sexually.

_____ 7. I can easily identify one person I'm attracted to above all others.

_____ 8. My parents had addictive tendencies.

_____ 9. I fantasize about an ideal partner who would know me and love me thoroughly.

_____ 10. I tend to view each new person (of the opposite sex) I meet as a potential conquest.

_____ 11. I tend to ignore the flaws in the person I'm in love with.

_____ 12. When I think about my childhood, I have unresolved issues that still cause me pain.

_____ 13. I think there's something wrong with me that makes me hard to love.

_____ 14. I often feel inadequate sexually.

_____ 15. I think I can change the flaws in the person I love.

_____ 16. I feel that I usually give in when others want something from me.

_____ 17. Sometimes I'm treated unfairly in a relationship, but it's worth it just to be loved.

_____ 18. I fantasize about an ideal lover who will give me great pleasure.

_____ 19. The person I'm in love with makes up for my shortcomings.

_____ 20. My romantic relationships tend to vacillate between love and hate.

_____ 21. When I am in a romantic relationship, I tend to let all of my other friendships drift away.

_____ 22. I feel most loved when I am involved in sexual intimacy.

_____ 23. I get extremely jealous when my partner shows interest in someone else.

_____ 24. I have recently suffered an emotional trauma that brought me great pain.

_____ 25. When I am in a loving relationship, I feel energized and powerful.

_____ 26. I often fantasize about having sex with people I see on TV or in the movies.

_____ 27. I feel physically ill if I have to be away from the one I love for a week or more.

_____ 28. When I am in a relationship, it tends to control my life.

Scoresheet

1	2	3	4
5	6	7	8
9	10	11	12
13	14	15	16
17	18	19	20
21	22	23	24
25	26	27	28

Column Totals:

(L)	(S)	(P)	(G)

Scoring

Put your answers in the appropriate spaces in the table and total the columns, top to bottom. Now you have four totals, labeled *L* ("love" addiction), *S* (sex addiction), *P* (addiction to a person), and *G* (general addictive factors). Let's take a closer look at what the numbers mean.

"LOVE" ADDICTION *(L)*

As you recall, "love" addiction is the compulsion to be in a relationship, the perceived need to be loved. It is often related to low self-esteem. The "love" addict feels a need to be with someone else in order to "be somebody." I put "love" in quotes because it's not real love such people crave, but the feeling of being in love.

45–49: You feel you need a romantic relationship to survive. This need can get you into trouble as you jump into a bad relationship just to be in *any* relationship. Read this book, but don't stop there. You may need to see a professional counselor.

39–44: You have a strong tendency toward "love" addiction. You have high expectations for romantic relationships and probably a low estimation of what you can accomplish on your own. You need to move toward more realistic understandings of both areas—and be careful about the relationships you're in.

32–38: You lean toward "love" addiction. It may not be an ongoing danger for you, but it's something to watch for, especially if you face a sudden trauma, such as a painful breakup or family crisis. Shoring up your self-esteem will prepare you for any rough times ahead.

25–31: It's not a problem, but be aware of any sudden changes in your attitude, perhaps brought about by a crisis. Especially if you score high in another area of relationship addiction, you could easily slide into a "love" addiction as well.

Below 25: You are below average on the danger scale. This doesn't seem to be a problem for you at this time.

SEX ADDICTION (S)

Although other books these days discuss sex addiction in conjunction with pornography and promiscuity, I focus on it *in relationships*. It may be manifested in those other ways, but how does it affect the relationships such a person is looking for or is presently in? Thus, the statements deal not with behavior but with feelings. The responses measure a *tendency* toward sex addiction rather than the actual playing out of it.

45–49: You are in trouble. You tend to confuse sex with love, and you seek to use others sexually to overcome your feelings of inadequacy. Besides reading this book, consider participating in a sex addiction support group and seeing a professional counselor.

39–44: You have a strong tendency toward sex addiction. You probably love and hate sex at the same time. You feel strong sexual impulses and sometimes try to fight them off. You need to work at defining sex and love as separate forces, and you need to strive to gain a healthy understanding of the opposite sex. Be careful about your present relationship if you're in one. Avoid temptation as much as possible.

32–38: You lean toward sex addiction. Be very careful about the stimuli you take in. Be aware of the messages from TV and movies, the music you listen to, the people you hang around with. Our whole society leans toward sex addiction. Don't let it take you for a ride.

25–31: It's not a problem, but watch for any sudden changes in your attitude, perhaps brought about by a crisis. Especially if you score high in another area of relationship addiction, you could find yourself in a sex addiction as well.

Below 25: You are below average on the danger scale. This doesn't seem to be a problem for you at this time.

ADDICTION TO A PERSON *(P)*

This addiction differs from the others in that it focuses on a specific person. If you are not presently seeing someone special, responding to these statements may have been hard. Perhaps you thought back to past relationships. So it's possible that you scored high here, even if you're not presently in an addictive relationship. But the high score would still show a tendency toward person-addiction.

43–49: You are almost certainly addicted to someone, or you are in extreme danger of falling into a person-addiction. You tend to look to this person for salvation, for identity, for purpose in life. Try to establish an identity of your own, apart from this person. You may need the help of a professional counselor to do so.

36–42: You have a strong tendency toward person-addiction. You tend to worship the person you're involved with, *or* you feel that this person could not live without you. (Person-addiction can go both ways—you need your partner, your partner needs you, you need to be needed, etc. If your situation is more one-sided, you may not score as high, but you may still have a problem.) You need to look for ways to break away, even subtly, and let you and the other person exist as independent people.

28–35: You lean toward person-addiction. (Because some of the statements measure caretaking, which may not apply in all cases, the score breakdown is lower—28 is an average score, but could still indicate a leaning.) Be careful about the relationships you get involved in or how you conduct your present relationship. Keep your eyes open to the foibles of your partner (and your own), and encourage your partner (and yourself) to make independent decisions from time to time.

23–27: It may not be a problem, but watch for growing dependency in a relationship. Work toward a mutuality, an interdependence in which both partners are strengthened as individuals, even as the two of you grow together.

Below 23: You are below average on the danger scale. This doesn't seem to be a problem for you at this time.

GENERAL ADDICTIVE FACTORS *(G)*

As we will see in our next chapter, the roots of relationship addiction go deep into our experience in growing up and with past relationships. These responses measure the existence of these factors. You may score high and still have few problems with addictions, but that would be rare. This score indicates your general susceptibility to relationship addiction.

45–49: You are a relationship addiction waiting to happen (if it hasn't happened already). A number of background and attitude factors are present that could easily lead you into addictive situations. Once again, professional counseling may help you deal with some of them.

39–44: You have a strong tendency toward relationship addiction. You need to work at resolving some of the issues from your childhood or from past relationships that are causing you pain. Especially if you recently had an emotional trauma, take the time to heal. It may be best not to be in a romantic relationship right now.

32–38: You lean toward relationship addiction of some kind. Several key factors are present. If you manage them well, you'll be fine. But be careful about bringing unresolved personal issues into your relationships.

25–31: You do not have significant background or attitude factors that would lead you into a relationship addiction. That does not mean you're scot-free. You may still succumb to momentary pressures.

Below 25: You are below average on the danger scale. This doesn't seem to be a problem for you at this time.

Obviously, your situation is unique. Use these numbers to get a general sense of your situation, but don't be enslaved by them. The test may break down at some point, or you may be an exception. But if you need help in a certain area, you probably know it already. This test just confirms it. And don't be alarmed if you score high in all areas. That is common. Addictive personalities often struggle in different areas. Use the findings of this test not to paralyze you with worry but to spur you to positive action.

Chapter Six

CASE STUDY: SCOTT

Scott is a caretaker. He takes care of others. He feels fulfillment when he is helping somebody. It's a good way to be, but it has its pitfalls. It's the classic tale of codependency—if he succeeds in nursing someone back to health, he's out of a job.

When Scott first came to me, he was involved in a relationship he had lots of questions about. It was wonderful; it was terrible. It was making him stronger and weaker. It was delighting him and depressing him. He wasn't sure what to do.

He had met Julie "by accident," he says. They were at a church retreat, and she thought he was someone else. They had lunch together and a long conversation that neither wanted to end. Scott was a leader in the church, affable and dedicated. Julie was a young mother, newly separated from her husband. In Scott, she found a listening ear and a warm heart. She unfolded a story of long-term emotional abuse by her husband. She was very, very needy.

The need was attractive to Scott, like a magnet. As he listened to the troubled soul, he was drawn in. He asked himself, How can I help? What can I do? How can I save this person from her distress?

Scott was no stranger to divorce. His parents had split up when he was young, and he knew firsthand the agony of alienation. An experience like that can damage a person or strengthen one. Even at a young age, a victim of divorce decides whether to be part of the problem or part of the solution. Scott decided to be part of the solution—and he's been a caretaker ever since.

A BLOSSOMING RELATIONSHIP

A friendship blossomed between the church leader and the estranged wife. Mother's Day was coming up. So she wouldn't feel neglected, Scott sent a card of encouragement.

Soon she was inviting him to dinner. Having come from a wealthy family, she had a comfortable life-style. Scott, a lifelong bachelor with a rather low-paying ministry-related job, appreciated her large, comfortable home. It was something he could get used to.

The dinners became more frequent. Their friendship intensified. She was sharing deep secrets of her life, neglect from her upbringing and betrayal by many of the men in her life. He was listening, understanding, caring. Even then, he was aware of a romantic undercurrent. He carried on a running monologue within himself: *This is not good. She's still married. This is tantamount to adultery. This is just not good.*

Friendly hugs turned into good-night kisses, which yielded to even greater intimacy. She overwhelmed him with her physical and emotional needs. She longed to be held, to be loved, to be sexually intimate with a man she cared about. He tried desperately to cling to his moral convictions.

By that time, Scott was convinced that Julie's marriage was beyond reconciliation. He believed in marriage and didn't want to be a party to her divorce. But she was still technically married, and that bothered him. Any romantic interaction was questionable at best. What's more, as a Bible-believing Christian, Scott believed in chastity before marriage. Although he allowed for certain casual stages of physical intimacy, he drew the line long before intercourse. Yet Julie kept pulling him across those lines.

She wanted—she "needed"—more of his physical attention. It became an issue between them. She had a way of winning arguments, though, and Scott kept easing his principles.

"It just snowballed," he says, looking back on it. "As we spent more time together, she desired more intimacy, and I just kept compromising, compromising, compromising."

Aware of his moral struggles, Scott stepped down from his church leadership position before anyone else knew there was a problem. Knowing that his Christian friends would disapprove, Scott would not talk about his relationship with Julie. And as he spent more and more time with her, he withdrew from his broad circle of friends.

While Scott was attracted to Julie's vulnerability, he also saw that when she had to be, she was quite strong and resourceful. Even though she was getting family pressure to go back to her husband, she was able to stand firm against it. Doing that was no easy task, considering the perceived power and wealth of her family.

That combination of strength and weakness was compelling to Scott. Julie was a dynamic woman, temporarily wounded by a tragedy. That was all the more reason for Scott to be there for her, to care for her, to restore her to a place of strength.

There was also the sense of "you and me against the world." Cult leaders know that they can cement the dedication of their followers if they portray themselves as gravely misunderstood by the outside world. The same holds true in relationships. The feeling that "I am the only one who really understands this person" will often bind the two fast together. Who else can the person turn to?

A prayer in the Psalms says, "The reproaches of those who reproach You have fallen on me" (Ps. 69:9), and the New Testament applies it to the Messiah. If Scott was playing "Messiah" here, he could have said this to Julie. By associating with her, he was taking her family's judgment on himself as well. He was also burning his bridges, alienating his friends. Julie became his whole world.

The divorce proceedings plodded on month after month, and

Scott's relationship with Julie plodded along, too. Every so often, Scott would come to terms with the unhealthiness of it. He would try to break it off. But she would react irrationally. "She was really an emotional basket case," he says. "I feared for her life." And so he stayed with her.

SECOND THOUGHTS

Scott had a good friend in Colorado, whose opinion he respected. With his support structure eroded at home, Scott consulted his friend to get perspective on the situation.

"Why are you in this relationship?" the friend asked.

"I don't know," Scott replied.

"You're telling me that it's unhealthy, it's driving you crazy, and it's ruining your friendships and your spiritual life. Why don't you just call it quits?"

"I don't know," Scott said. "I just can't."

"There's something else there," the friend said. "There's a reason somewhere."

What was the mystery reason? Romantics might say that the lovers were "meant" to be together. It might defy all logic, but go for it! Unfortunately, that thinking gets a lot of people in trouble. It seems to me that the "something else" holding Scott to Julie (and Julie to Scott) was addiction, pure and simple. Julie needed Scott to fill the gaps in herself that were left by her failed marriage. Scott needed to be needed by Julie. That was where he derived his purpose.

The roller coaster continued. A year and a half into the relationship, *Julie* called it quits. She was frustrated with the boundaries Scott was trying to place on their relationship. It was "hurting" her, she said. She needed more.

There it was, his ticket out—right? But Scott was addicted, too. It hurt him to be without her. The idea that she needed more than he could give was devastating. He was a failure.

Within weeks Julie began to date other people. Maybe she wanted to convince herself she was still worth being wined and dined. Maybe she feared Scott was taking her for granted.

Maybe she sincerely wanted to try something new. Nonetheless, she was back with Scott within a few months. And things went on as they had—only Scott may have made a few more compromises.

PERSONAL STUFF

A year later, Scott felt stagnant. He was aware that he had forgone his personal growth to attend to Julie's needs. He needed to restore himself. Once again, he tried to break up.

"There are things in me I need to work on," he told her. "This relationship isn't helping either of us. We aren't happy. I need to go and work on my stuff. I have to sort some things out. Maybe then I can come back and we'll be better off."

She couldn't take it. For weeks she cried constantly. She couldn't keep up her responsibilities and couldn't even care for her young son properly. When Scott stopped taking her phone calls, she called Scott's family and friends, begging them to change his mind.

When she got through to Scott, she said, "I cannot live without you. I want to help you work through your stuff. We can compromise . . . maybe cut back on how often we're together. Take the time you need, but don't shut me out of your life."

Scott backed down. And he slipped right back into the routine. Every night at her place for dinner, weekends spent there, then vacations together. He didn't get much chance to work on his stuff. He was a full-fledged addict.

He did take another trip to Colorado, though. Maybe Scott was seeking strength to follow through on a breakup, but his friend tried another tactic. "Why don't you marry her?" the friend asked.

Scott was stunned. Julie's divorce would soon be final, and he had thought about this possibility. But why would his friend suggest it?

"Look," the friend explained, "I could tell you to break up once and for all, but would you? From everything you've said to me, sure, you should break up. It's unhealthy. But you're not breaking up with her. You don't really want to. So, if that's the way it is, why don't you marry her? Just get out of this limbo."

Shortly after Scott returned, the divorce became final. They continued to have some problems. She had some problems with her son, which caused her great stress for a time, and that drew Julie and Scott closer. But otherwise they fought frequently. She was very critical of him. She seemed to be pulling away somewhat. And he wanted her more than ever.

On Valentine's Day he proposed. She turned him down. A week later, she wanted to talk.

"It's over," she said. "I want to be friends with you . . . but just friends. I hope you're not mad at me."

Mad? Why should he be mad?

Try "devastated."

The "just friends" arrangement made things worse. She still invited him to dinner. She still asked him for help with her son and work around the house, fixing the car and so on.

Was she indicating a desire to restore their relationship, to get back together? No, she insisted. They were still broken up. She explained starkly, "My love for you is dead. I'm in a different place now than you are." Obviously, both of them were having trouble redefining the relationship.

DEVASTATION

That's when Scott came to me. The change in the relationship utterly confused him. He was like a recovering alcoholic working as a bartender, feeding his addiction with touch and smell, though not with taste. Julie seemed oblivious to his plight. She felt sorry for him when she saw his anguish, but there wasn't much she could do—short of reviving the romance.

She had changed. She had recovered from her position of extreme need. She didn't need Scott anymore. She wanted to fulfill other needs that Scott couldn't touch. She was truly "in a different place." She was trying to maintain the friendship she enjoyed with Scott while staying free from a romantic relationship with him. Why couldn't he be happy with that?

Julie had become the strong one. She had previously controlled him with her need. Now she was setting the boundaries of the relationship, and Scott soon realized that he couldn't change them.

"I'm in the midst of trying to accept it," he says now, a few months after the breakup. "If you did an autopsy on me today, you'd open me up and find my heart in a thousand pieces. It feels like every day I'm having a heart attack. I'm not sleeping well. I'm not eating well. Most mornings I lose my breakfast before I go to work. I'm devastated."

Shortly after Scott came to me, I urged him to go cold turkey. By continuing to see Julie, he was prolonging the pain and in danger of resuming his addiction. He talked with her about it, and they agreed to avoid each other for a time. That withdrawal has obviously had a powerful effect on Scott. The physical symptoms alone are frightening, but he will recover.

The emotional and spiritual recovery will take longer. "I feel like I failed," he says. "Even though we weren't married, I feel like I was divorced." Scott still has the gifts that have made him popular in the past, but his self-esteem is shattered. He gave up his support structure, his circle of friends, and now he'll have to try to restore the relationships. For three and a half years he drew his sense of self-worth from his ability to meet Julie's needs. He felt very, very important to her. But now, her change toward him pulls the rug out from under him. What good is he?

And that intensifies other problems in his life—dissatisfaction with his job, evaluation of his life ambitions, a certain spiritual reordering.

"We were best friends," he says. "We had great communication. And that's the hardest thing about it. I not only lost my lover, I lost my best friend. Right now, when I'm struggling with my personal issues, that's the hardest thing for me, that my best friend isn't there."

It's hard for Scott to accept, but not being with Julie is the best thing for him. He needs to find other survival strategies. He needs to find other friends to work through these issues with. He needs to rebuild his self-esteem through other activities.

"The funny thing is that I wanted out for so long. Every day for a year or more, I would go home at night and say, 'What am I doing? This is ridiculous! I need to get out of this.' Now I'm just amazed that I'm so frustrated. I'm thinking, *Why am I struggling with this so much? Why does this hurt so much?* I just don't understand why I care so much and why I'm addicted to wanting to be with her."

EVALUATION

You've just read about a textbook case of relationship addiction. Many of the characteristics discussed in chapters three and four surface in this account.

Compulsion. Even when Scott decided that he *had* to break off the relationship, he couldn't. "Something else" was holding him there.

Attempt to rescue. Scott was a rescuer from the beginning. That's rooted deep in his nature. Perhaps he learned it young, as a child of divorce, wanting desperately to care for his needy parents. That's Scott's whole gig—he *understands* and cares for people in need. That's what he does for a living—help people—and in his personal life. Julie needed care, and Scott provided it.

Rose-colored glasses. Scott is still speaking of all the good things that Julie did for him, boosting his self-esteem and so on. The fact is that she crushed his self-esteem. (I don't mean to attack her in this. She was clawing her way back to emotional health in the wake of her divorce. But Scott would have benefited by keeping his eyes open to the whole reality of that relationship.)

Exclusivity. Scott gave up many, many friends—some who disapproved of the relationship, others he just didn't have time for anymore.

Jealousy. Scott was very sensitive about his low earnings and jealous of men who could take Julie out in style.

Continuing dysfunction. Scott is a child of divorce, and there are some dysfunctional issues in Julie's history. Both were wounded souls continuing the pattern.

Overdependence. Julie seemed to go through a normal process of divorce recovery. She depended on Scott a great deal to begin with, but she gained strength and self-confidence over a few years, with a few relapses. I would suggest that the early dependence was overdone. (That's why I counsel newly divorced people to avoid new romances for about two years; they tend to overdepend on their new partners.)

Scott, on the other hand, depended on Julie for practical matters, such as meals and companionship, and for his self-esteem. The practical overdependence was bad enough—and it has made the breakup especially jolting since his whole life-style is changed—but the emotional overdependence was even more dangerous. Scott was defining himself as a need-meeter, specifically as *Julie's* need-meeter. But as Julie gained health, Scott became obsolete. And when he was no longer needed, he had no more purpose in life.

Love-hate cycle. The ups and downs of the relationship are evident and typical of an addictive relationship in which the emotional stakes are so high. As Julie went through the bumpy ride of divorce recovery, Scott went along. He was there when she needed him, and he was rejected when she didn't. His situation is not unlike that of a teenager's parent, helping someone to maturity but often rejected in the process. It is important for a teenager to learn to live independently, but that usually occurs awkwardly and painfully. The same was true for Julie. At times she needed him desperately, but at other times she needed *not* to need him. That was necessary but hard for him to take.

Weakening. At the beginning of the relationship, any onlooker would say that Scott was the strong one; Julie was a basket case. But those roles flip-flopped. As Julie regained confidence (thanks partly to Scott), she became the strong one in the relationship, deciding when and how she needed Scott. Now Julie is doing fine, while Scott suffers. She feels sympathy for Scott's pain and would like to help him, but she will not allow herself to be dragged into it again. (That's a good choice; trying to help him cope with it would just continue the addictive cycle.)

Scott was clearly weakened by the relationship. And Julie?

Was she strengthened? Perhaps. But I would suggest that her healing would have occurred faster if she had not been romantically involved with Scott. If Scott had kept his distance, helping her as a friend and minister, he would have had a more positive effect on her life.

Scott will heal, though the first few months will be tough. He and Julie *must* go cold turkey, and that has been difficult for them so far. His healing cannot begin until he slams the door on the romance with Julie.

He needs to redefine himself. He can no longer attribute value to himself only when he is meeting someone's need. He needs to bolster his self-esteem. Servanthood is great; it's a Christian calling. But we are valuable servants to God even if no one else wants our services. Scott desperately needs to learn that.

_____ *Chapter Seven* _____

THE ROOTS OF ADDICTIVE RELATIONSHIPS

Why do I do this to myself? you ask, staring into your morning coffee. The passion that clouded your thinking the night before has now passed, and you examine your life in the clear light of day.

You've done this before, haven't you? Previous relationships have shown the same symptoms. Overinvolvement. You allow yourself to think less of yourself. You *need* this relationship, and if you don't have it, you'll just die. You've put all your eggs in one basket, and now the basket's about to drop. Or the eggs are just rotting there. You feel trapped in a bad relationship or a bad cycle. When will you ever learn? You wouldn't know a healthy relationship if it knocked on your door with flowers in hand. You sip your coffee to wake up to a new day that will turn out just like yesterday, only one crank further on the downward spiral.

Why do I do this to myself?

There *are* reasons. You may be interested to know that your addictive tendencies come from somewhere. And if you can understand their source, perhaps you can change some basic behaviors and attitudes. Perhaps you can break out of this prison.

With addiction, stopping the drinking or going on a diet will only solve the symptom of the problem. Dissolving a relationship or moving away might be a good course of action for a person-addiction, but the solution doesn't stop there. Chances are, your addictive tendencies will surface in other ways, perhaps other relationships. You need to go back to the roots of your addiction and seek a permanent solution through treatment of root issues.

In *Addicted to "Love,"* Stephen Arterburn uses the image of water cascading down a mountain. Addictive tendencies are something like this, he says. If you dam up one path that the water takes, it will find another. His point is to show how the different types of addiction are related, and it's true that often a person will stop one addiction only to start another.

But if I could change that picture a bit, let's say we go to the source of that water, perhaps a mountain lake. And let's build some conduits, with pipes or natural stream beds, and let's channel that water down the mountain so that it can serve a useful purpose below. It may be a losing battle if we try to dam up one path after another, but if we go to the source, we can alleviate the destruction and make some good things happen.

You get it, don't you? We need to confront our addictive tendencies at the source. And then perhaps we can interrupt the destructive patterns and establish new conduits for that energy.

Experience and research have led psychologists and researchers to hypothesize several reasons that people tend toward addictive relationships. These can be classified into three general categories: (1) genetic tendencies; (2) family-of-origin issues; and (3) emotional vulnerability. Let's take a closer look at each one of these roots of addiction.

GENETIC TENDENCIES

Scientists differ on this issue, but some have suggested that a certain gene makes a person prone to addiction. Genes may also determine our personalities and preferred style of relating to others.

In our group of people struggling with addictive relationships, six of them had alcoholic parents. Was that just a coincidence?

Since leading that group, I have made a conscious effort to inquire about the hereditary backgrounds of all of my addictive clients, and my informal research has determined that at least 80 percent of them came from some type of family addiction, whether it was substance abuse, sex addiction, workaholism, or gambling.

Of course, my figures hardly make up a scientific study. But they are not too far off the more formal research cited by the American Medical Association (AMA). Listen to this news release:

> The biological approach took a big step forward . . . when researchers reported the identification of a specific gene that may play a key role in some forms of alcoholism as well as other addictions. Of the alcoholics they studied, *77 percent* had the identified gene. The discovery, announced by researchers at the University of Texas and UCLA, is a gene linked to the receptors for dopamine, a brain chemical involved in the sensation of pleasure. Such discoveries, scientists say, herald biological markers that may one day make possible early identification of those most at risk of becoming addicted, allowing more effective prevention and treatment.

The "biological approach" mentioned is one side of an ongoing controversy between nature and nurture. This feud underlies several modern issues. While I am very interested in the continuing biological research, let me say that I find great problems with a *completely* biological approach to addiction.

Here's my gripe. It's easy to use biology as an excuse: "I just couldn't help myself! It's just the way I am!" People can develop a fatalistic approach to a problem: "I'll never defeat it. It's in my genes."

Even with recent biological research, these are invalid assumptions. Our genes may give us a tendency toward certain behaviors, but we must still choose what to do. In fact, part of our healing must include taking full responsibility for our thoughts and behaviors. Unhealthy relationships are still unhealthy, and we still need to get out of them, even if we have to fight against our biology.

And even with the biological data, establishing a solid cause-and-effect link is difficult. For example, if we take the most common form of addiction, alcohol abuse, we can reason that the alcoholic also neglected the children from time to time. Therefore, what caused the daughter to seek unhealthy relationships as an adult—the alcoholic gene pool or the parental neglect? The best answer is probably, to some degree, both. We just don't know the degree to which each factor drove her to find relationships to numb the pain of her empty life.

The medical evidence

Let's take a closer look at that biological evidence. Though it is not conclusive, a growing body of research supports a genetic link for addictions. Most of the research has been done on alcohol and drug abusers, but the literature also mentions common problems with the way addicts handle their feelings, stress, and depression.

Our bodies naturally produce enzymes called endorphins, druglike substances that make us feel good. They are released to the brain when we enjoy a beautiful spring day or when we sit down to a favorite meal or when we see a loved one. According to Carolyn Johnson in *Understanding Alcoholism*, for addicts, however, these hormones may not be released in the same way, and when they are released, there may be fewer of them. This release of hormones affects not only the way they metabolize alcohol but also their ability to control their appetite, their sense of well-being, the way they overcome depression, and the levels of their physiological desires.

These findings have dramatic implications for addicts. If they are true, they explain why some people struggle so much with drinking, but to others, it is no big deal; why one person gives up cigarettes in one day, but another agonizes for a lifetime; and why one person finds the entire reason for living in an addictive relationship, but another maintains a healthy balance with a partner.

For people struggling with addictions, there has to be more than willpower involved. Some very strong people become like infants in the grip of an addictive substance. And it can't be just a matter of making foolish choices. Some very smart people repeat similar mistakes when it comes to dating relationships. Apparently, some other factor—nature, nurture, or both—stacks the deck against certain people.

But what determines that one individual will become an alcoholic, another a chronic gambler, and another a love addict?

Our "drug of choice"

No research indicates a genetic propensity toward any *particular* addiction, that is, not yet. Our technology is not that refined, but perhaps someday this, too, will be determined. The same underlying motivations, the same search for meaning, the same need to block our pain, and perhaps even similar genetic irregularities may be present in all addicts, but our "drugs of choice" may be very different.

Why is it that more men struggle with drug and alcohol addictions, but more women have addictive relationships? Why do men have a greater problem with sex addiction, but more women are treated for emotional dependencies? There is strong evidence for both sex differences and personality differences in determining someone's drug of choice.

In this regard, I suspect a much stronger interplay between our inherited tendencies and environmental factors. In other words, we may be born with the addictive personality type, but our upbringing, experiences, and personalities may determine the type of addiction we combat.

Our personality types

Is there a personality type that is more prone to addictive relationships? I believe there is. That doesn't mean other people are automatically free from unhealthy relationships. Even the strongest among us are susceptible. But I have seen a greater imbalance among individuals with *dependent* personalities. Such people are followers rather than leaders. They love to serve others. They tend to be very nurturing and caring in relationships.

Is this wrong? Is this personality type "bad"? No, not at all. If that's the way your personality is, that's how God made you—it's not a mistake. (And the Bible frequently praises those who love to serve and care for others.) But do you need to be more cautious with the relationships you form? Absolutely! In the same way, the natural leaders and "take charge" people among us need to be careful that they don't dominate and manipulate others. They might be susceptible to a power addiction.

The world needs both personality types. Otherwise where would our nurses, counselors, and loyal employees come from? And where would our salespeople, marketing gurus, and corporate presidents come from?

Once again, let's look at the evidence from our original group:

- Dawn is a nurse at the local hospital.
- Margie is a second-grade teacher in a public school.
- Joy is the secretary for her pastor.
- Laurie is an office manager for six salespeople.
- David is studying to be a social worker.
- Ginnie has had a series of clerical jobs and presently is a secretary to a financial advisor.
- Karen is a clerical worker who was verbally and emotionally abused before her marriage fell apart.

What other personality types form addictive relationships? Besides being nurturing and dependent in relationships, these individuals tend to be more self-conscious, self-deficient, and conventional/conforming.

Self-conscious. They are very sensitive to criticism and may frequently feel that others don't like them, though they may have no concrete evidence upon which to base that feeling. They are nervous in public or in the spotlight of attention. They think about themselves a lot, constantly second-guessing themselves: "Should I have said that? Maybe I should have done it differently."

To find relief from this self-absorption, such people try to find partners they can pour their lives into. Within these relationships, they attain a certain degree of acceptance and are at least distracted from their self-doubt.

Self-deficient. These people tend to have a low self-image and to struggle with guilt and shame. They feel unworthy around others; therefore, they seek relationships with those who are considered (by friends and family) "beneath" them. They spend much of their relational time trying to prove themselves and measure up to other people's standards. Whenever a relationship fails, they tend to blame themselves and identify some personal weakness.

In extreme cases, they may engage in self-punishment. They may put themselves in self-defeating situations just to prove to themselves that they really are worthless and deserve punishment. The behavior may be unconscious.

Conventional/conforming. Unlike those who struggle with other addictions, the relationship addict tends to be quite conventional and to follow the crowd. This personality trait may be a factor in determining the type of addiction someone chooses. Archibald Hart says in *Healing Life's Hidden Addictions* that substance abusers tend to be risk takers, unconventional and rebellious; relationship addicts are very different. The root insecurity of relationship addicts leads them to seek approval rather than escape. Being alone is awful. Standing out in a crowd is shameful. Such people must be part of a group or attached to another person.

If you have one of these personality types, you're not doomed to addictive relationships. But you're susceptible to them. If you do not fit into these types, it does not mean you're not susceptible. It just means you're not *as* susceptible as those who are.

A complex synergy leads to relationship addiction. Genetic factors and the personalities we're born with provide a few pieces of the puzzle. For the rest, we need to consult the nurture side of things.

FAMILY-OF-ORIGIN ISSUES

We've made a pretty good case for the theory that genetic tendencies form the roots of addiction, but now we need to look at a second factor that can act just as strongly: family background and experiences.

What is it about the way people were raised that could cause them to seek unhealthy relationships in adult life? In general, I have observed that people who struggle with addictive relationships grew up in a home where they saw no healthy relationships or where there was some type of love deprivation.

Love deprivation

Human beings could be deprived of proper love and attention for many reasons. Love deprivation may affect

- children who did not properly bond with one or both parents in their earliest years of life due to extended hospitalization, foster care, or inconsistent caregivers.
- children who bonded early but then lost contact with either parent or both parents during childhood due to death, separation, or the inability of the parent(s) to care for the children. This inability to parent can apply to those who were alcoholic, drug addicted, mentally ill, extremely dysfunctional, or chronically absent.
- youngsters and teens who had little nurturance from one or

both parents due to a lack of love, frequent absence, neglect, or abuse.

- teens, young adults, and adults who have experienced the lack of or loss of love from a series of significant persons in their lives.

In our group, as the participants discussed their family backgrounds, we discovered the common thread of alcoholism and dysfunction, as mentioned earlier. But along with that family background came the obvious neglect and sometimes deprivation that go hand in hand with specific dysfunctions. Several described absent or uncaring fathers they were constantly trying to please, though they received very little acknowledgment. Others spoke of mothers who were cold, distant, or uncaring. Whichever the case, the result was the same. Feeling unloved and uncared for as a child led them to seek love desperately as a teen or an adult.

In our group, David talked about his parents' separation when he was about ten years old and their eventual divorce. But the deprivation began long before his dad's final departure. As long as he can remember, his mother was in and out of the hospital. Later, as a teen, he found out that she was in a mental hospital, but as a preschooler, he knew only that his mother was gone. He was left with baby-sitters and relatives so that his father could work. And even when his mother was home, she was chronically depressed, which meant she had little energy for nurturing her son.

David cannot remember a time when he felt secure and consistently loved. Instead, he felt great emotional distance from his mother and abandonment from his father. In adult life, David seeks to find love wherever he can find it, but as stated earlier, the women he dates never seem to measure up. He's attracted to them, and he pursues them, but he can't trust that they will love him unconditionally and that they will not abandon him. So he usually rejects them before they have the chance to leave him.

Ginnie's pattern of addiction seems different from that of other group members, but the seeds of addiction were very similar. Ginnie described her father as being "unobtainable." He separated from the family several times while Ginnie was growing up, but even when he was home, he paid no attention to her—except when he had been drinking and came to her room at night. Ginnie constantly tried to get his attention by following him around the house, then by asking him lots of questions, and later by excelling at school; but the result was always the same. He was not interested in her. Even as a teenager, when Ginnie swore she would not allow him to affect her life, she had an unquenchable desire to have him approve of her and to show it. Today as a thirty-something adult, she is still seeking his love.

She has compensated, however, by finding a way to get *other* men to notice her. Since high school, Ginnie found that she had a very powerful influence over men—even men her father's age.

Ginnie learned how to dress and act provocatively. She soon began to act on her sexual impulses, and she discovered a whole new world of male attention was opened up to her. Men not only noticed her but also sought her out and flocked around her. Getting the attention was very reassuring, but it did not last. Each time she thought she found a special relationship, she soon felt rejection; her phone calls weren't returned, or she was stood up for a date. The rejection made Ginnie even more determined to find acceptance. And she always led with what she thought was her greatest asset. She knew she could appeal to men sexually.

It wasn't so much the sex that she was interested in. In fact, she claimed that she didn't even enjoy that part of it. She merely wanted the attention, the holding, the affection, the kind words. Ginnie became quite good at going to a club or a bar and going home with whomever she chose. When she was out with her girlfriends, she unconsciously competed for the attention of any of the men who came around—and she usually got it. Her behavior obviously alienated many of her friends and drove her even deeper into her empty life of addictive love.

Ginnie and David are very different, but both are examples of persons whose parents have imprinted a love deficiency onto their children. This imprint can follow them for the rest of their lives until they find some way to fill the void.

Finding the love we crave

It's a simple equation. If we don't get enough love as children, we seek it as adults. The problem might be an absentee father, a distant or an uncaring mother, abusive parents, or emotionally neglectful loved ones. In all of these cases, children grow up without the proper basis for loving relationships and without the proper role models of unconditional love. Having unhealthy adult relationships is not always the result, but that's the tendency.

Sometimes the unmet needs from childhood drive us to medicate the pain of our empty lives through drugs, alcohol, sex, or gambling. These temporary fixes help for a while, but when they fail us (and they always do), we try something else, perhaps something more socially acceptable—work, food, religion, or a relationship. But we soon find that no object, substance, or relationship has the ability to satisfy the void of an empty life, a life without the security of unconditional love. (Unconditional love is discussed in more detail in chapter 12.)

Exploration of the family of origin and pain from the past can be a tedious process. The goal is not to find an excuse for self-pity or even to find someone else to blame. The goal is to figure out what went wrong and how to fix it. Early childhood imprints make powerful impressions on us. To overcome their influence, we must recognize what was wrong in childhood, understand how it affects our lives, learn what we can from the experience, and determine to change the future for ourselves and our children.

EMOTIONAL VULNERABILITY

A third reason people enter addictive relationships is their emotional vulnerability, usually because of some loss or specific need in their lives. These people may have grown up in loving homes with parents who were not alcoholic or addictive, and yet for a period of time they become very susceptible to addictive relationships.

I know firsthand because it happened to me.

I grew up in a loving home where no addiction was present. Other than puppy love in junior and senior high, I would have to classify my love relationships as being fairly healthy. I certainly had no tendency toward addiction, that is, until I experienced a divorce after four years of marriage. The divorce sent me into an emotional tailspin that lasted at least three years. I felt empty and quite lost. I actually felt as if part of me were missing, as if I had a large hole in my chest. My immediate desire was to find a quick way to fill the hole in my chest.

Most people believe that the best solution is to find someone else as quickly as possible: "What you need now is a romance to take your mind off your troubles." How many times have you heard that on TV or in real life? How many times have you *said* that? But the truth is, that prescription merely leads to an addictive relationship—one that is based solely on my need for affirmation, my emptiness, and my desire to be loved again.

In the wake of my divorce, I got involved with a woman who met my needs. Well, she met my *immediate* needs, the needs on the surface. She was someone to be with, someone to care for me, someone to cook my meals.

Our romance was doomed from the start because it was a need-based relationship. It was lopsided. As long as I was hurting, she could nurse me back to health. But as I regained my emotional strength, there was no more basis for the relationship. I believe that my recovery stalled for a while as I figured out what to do about my new dependency. (Why get healthy when there's someone to take care of you?) When we finally did muster the strength to be honest with each other, we broke up, amid great pain.

I needed, and other emotionally vulnerable people need, to allow the wounds to heal slowly, to become whole again. Just as a broken arm needs to be put in a cast, so our hearts need to be immobilized so that we don't try to use them again before they are completely healed. And as with that broken arm, if we insist on trying to love again with a broken or wounded heart, it will hurt all the more. If we continue to try to use it anyway, it's liable to heal crooked.

In our culture, divorce is the most common cause of what we

might call *catastrophic* emotional vulnerability. The vulnerability is not a chronic condition based on genetics or upbringing, but something has befallen you that makes you temporarily needy. Although divorce often brings a host of legal and social complications, other romantic breakups can be nearly as serious emotionally. Yet often the catastrophe occurs in an entirely different corner of your life. Perhaps a parent or other loved one dies. Perhaps you lose your job. Perhaps you are forced to move to a new area. A mid-life crisis may be enough to make you vulnerable to addictive relationships. If you're a woman, you may hear—and be distressed by—the ticking of your biological clock. If you're a man, you may be bored with your life and feeling like you haven't accomplished your ambitions. You need something to boost your ego!

Whatever the catastrophe, it often brings a temptation to seek healing in a new romance. From my experience as a counselor specializing in divorce recovery, I can tell you flat out: that's exactly the wrong place to find healing. A new romance is likely to make you *more* vulnerable, and it may rip your heart out. Even in the best situation, it is likely to delay the healing process by shielding you from the painful issues you must face.

After I gave a talk on these issues at a seminar, a man came up to me and asked, "Could this broken heart thing have anything to do with the fact that since my divorce, I've been in seven relationships in five years? All of them seemed so right, but each ended disastrously. I'd begun to think I really was running into some unusually unloving women, but now I'm wondering if there isn't something wrong with me."

I responded, "How long after your divorce did you wait before you started dating again?"

"Oh, it was a long time," the man answered. "At least three or four months."

"And how long have you ever gone without being in a relationship with someone?" I asked.

Once again he replied, "At least three or four months."

I then encouraged him to stop dating, to take the time to go back and work through the issues of his broken marriage, and to become comfortable with himself. I knew that the man had a wounded heart. If he didn't stop trying to use it, it was bound to continue hurting, and it was probably starting to heal crookedly.

The catastrophes that can bring about emotional vulnerability usually shake our sense of *security* and *significance*. Psychologist Larry Crabb proposes that these are our two greatest emotional needs. They can be just as strong as our biological needs to eat and sleep.

I knew a young man who was struggling with dissatisfaction in a dead-end job. He did not feel significant. A young woman in his church had just been through a divorce, and she had two young children. She desperately needed security. You could probably guess what happened. They got together for an on-again, off-again romance that held them in an addictive grip for a couple of years.

He provided her some security. It was great for her to know that someone loved her. And she made him feel significant. But that's about all they did for each other. In many other ways, their affair was unhealthy. They compromised principles, drifted away from God, ditched other friendships, and often fought with each other.

Note the irony. Healthy relationships provide security and significance. But in our desperate attempt to find these things, we often end up in unhealthy relationships that rob us of these very things. We need to seek balance. It often happens as it did with the couple I just mentioned: one's security is another's significance. He felt important for being her anchor in tough times. She felt secure because he drew his significance from her. But her need to feel more significance threatened his. And when he needed security, she couldn't provide it. Their relationship was seriously tilted.

Serious relationships need to provide security and significance—and a host of other things. You may have no family history of addiction, and your upbringing may be splendid, but a sudden emotional jolt in adulthood can knock you into some unwise decisions. Take your time. Heal slowly. And when you are ready to enter a new romance, maintain balance.

_____ *Chapter Eight* _____

CASE STUDY: BONNIE

Bonnie came to me troubled about a dating relationship she could not shake. Somewhere within her, she knew it was unhealthy, but she could not summon the strength to break it off. That's why she was in my office.

Frequently, I find deeper issues in people's lives, ongoing unhealthy patterns. It's like the guy who goes to the doctor with a sore throat and ends up in the hospital for three weeks with some tropical disease. The presenting problem is often just the tip of the iceberg. The underlying needs are more titanic. Bonnie was such a case.

"Every relationship I've been in has been a mess," Bonnie told me. "I don't think I've been in a normal one yet." That made me start digging into her history.

She was the middle child in her family. One older brother and an older sister went through school ahead of her and made their marks. They were stars—athletes, scholars, class leaders. Bonnie was ordinary by comparison. And the comparisons were frequently made. "I didn't have a chance," she said, looking back on those days. And her younger sister always seemed to get more attention as the "baby" of the family.

Her great love was music—she sang beautifully—but her parents pressed her to do something more practical. Music was fine for a hobby, but she would have to make a living somehow. Bonnie wished she could apply her talents more, but instead of arguing, she complied with their wishes. Besides, she was sure they knew what was best for her. What could she possibly know? "I had zero self-esteem," she told me.

ROUND ONE: CHRIS

Bonnie went to a Christian college and began to blossom a bit outside her parents' home. Though she was still rather shy, she dated several young men. "If you dated the same person more than a couple of times," she explained, "people would begin to link you romantically with that person." So the guys just dated her a couple of times, then moved on. But then Chris came along.

He was a whirlwind, showing her attention, showering her with gifts. He wasn't wealthy, but she was his queen. Even in those early dates, there were conflicts. He had a bad temper, and he would sometimes snap at her. But she tended to excuse the episodes—after all, he was spending so much on her, he had to be in love with her. "Besides," she reasoned, "he was probably the best I could ever get." She had struggled for so long with her self-image that with all the attention, she found herself feeling better than she ever had before. The feeling had to be love. She knew she wanted more of it.

Yes, Chris was an authority figure. That was the plan, as Bonnie had learned from her parents' example and from her personal Bible study. Men had the authority over their wives, over their children. She would be passing from her father's authority to her husband's. And Chris was already taking control.

Bonnie's parents had some reservations about Chris, but Bonnie didn't want to hear them. They had caught him in some lies.

Her friends were worried about his temper, but Bonnie felt trapped. She married Chris.

Mission impossible

"He talked me into quitting school and working to put him through," Bonnie told me. "That was how trusting I was. He knew I wanted to be a missionary, so he decided we would be missionaries. For that he would need a degree—I wouldn't."

They decided—well, *he* decided—they'd serve the Lord in France, not far from Paris. They were appointed by a mission board for a church-planting project, and they toured churches to raise support. It was Bonnie's dream. Her brother and sisters had married well and gotten good jobs. She was one-upping them; she was a *missionary,* the best job a Christian could have. She feared it was all too good to be true. She was right.

When they got to France, Chris dropped his pretenses. He had always been a model Christian, in public anyway. He was quick to quote Bible verses and give pious answers. But he dropped the act. He let Bonnie know he was not interested in serving the Lord at all. He wanted to evade the draft and see the world. She was stunned.

Chris played a game, sending prayer letters back home with news of an unresponsive mission field while reveling in the Parisian night life and developing a pornography addiction. Bonnie was trapped in a foreign country; she was pregnant and financially dependent. So she felt she had to cover for him.

Chris kept trying to appease Bonnie with gifts. They lived in a nice house and drove a nice car, but he was a fraud and she knew it. "There was no emotion," she told me. "Despite all the gifts, he felt nothing for me."

The dishonesty also bothered her deeply. She was furious with him for his deception, and she felt guilty for joining in deceiving the folks back home. One day she found his briefcase full of pornographic pictures. She taped them to the refrigerator. "There!" she said. "If that's what you want, there they are! Don't try to hide them!"

And then she found evidence that he was being unfaithful to

her. She confronted him with her evidence, but he naturally denied everything. She felt unable to push the issue. As evidence and tension mounted, she refused to sleep with him. He stayed in the basement, coming and going as he pleased.

When their three-year term was up, Bonnie insisted that she could not go on. They would have to resign from the mission board. Chris wanted to continue the charade, but she refused and they returned to the States. Yet Chris never admitted his problems. "He told our supporting churches that I was homesick and had to come back," she said.

So she bore the blame for Chris's moral failings. She had made an attempt at a colossal spiritual achievement—being a missionary—but she couldn't hack it. Once again, in the eyes of her church and her family, she didn't measure up.

In addition, the cloud of a broken marriage was hanging over her. She tried to live with Chris for as long as possible because of her commitment to God and to her wedding vows. But it didn't work. She feared at one point that he was molesting their daughter. She knew he would deny everything again, and she didn't know what to do. She finally separated from her husband, but he demanded visitation rights. She talked with her pastor about the molestation; he "freaked out," she said later, and was no help. Finally, Bonnie contacted a social service agency that stepped in and stopped the visitation. Chris was upset. With his characteristic temper tantrums, he threatened Bonnie with violence. She moved away.

And yet she was still officially married to him. Her church didn't believe in divorce, her family didn't believe in divorce, and though it was clear that the whole thing was a bad mistake, Bonnie didn't believe in divorce, either. So for another several years she was in limbo—separated but not divorced.

Her instinct was to go back to her parents, but they insisted she try to make it on her own. So there she was, without a full college education, working at a make-ends-meet job she didn't enjoy, caring for a daughter by herself, having failed (or so she thought) as a wife, as a daughter, as a missionary, as a Christian.

Eventually, Chris divorced her; he wanted to get remarried.

ROUND TWO: STEVE

About that time, Round Two began. A man in Bonnie's church began showing her attention. It was nice. After fifteen years of being put down by her husband, and even more years of not feeling valued by her family, in his presence she felt like somebody. Once again she found someone who would build her self-image.

Steve met some needs in her life. She was weak emotionally. Though her marriage had been all but dissolved for a decade, the divorce was still hard to take. It was a final failure. All that time she had been praying for Chris's repentance and restoration, but they weren't going to happen. The anger, frustration, and self-hate boiled within her.

In Steve, Bonnie found a calming influence, a good friend, some new confidence. She was a bit uneasy when the relationship became romantic. It was all too soon, she felt. Besides, she still wasn't sure what she believed about dating again after a divorce. But Steve was persistent, and she craved the attention.

He wasn't wealthy enough to wine and dine her, but he showered her with attention, and that was a commodity she longed for. Steve was a leader in her church, a Sunday school teacher and deacon, so she assured herself that the relationship must be okay.

Steve started to push her for more physical intimacy, far more than she felt was morally acceptable. He was talking about marriage, and he seemed especially interested in moving in to her spacious home. Suddenly, she felt used and disillusioned once again. "He was a fake," she told me, "just interested in meeting his physical and material needs. He didn't really care about me or my daughter." If she couldn't trust a Sunday school teacher, who could she trust?

Bonnie lacked the courage to end the relationship with a face-to-face conversation. She would try, but his calming words would seduce her again. "Who knows how long I would have gone on like that?" she confessed later. "But finally, I moved away." She went back to the area where her parents lived. The romance was left behind.

ROUND THREE: TED

She was back in her parents' neighborhood. They were back in her life. She was their child again, thirty-five years old but now divorced. "They treated me like a little girl," she explained to me. She sometimes resented it, but she also accepted it. She let them make decisions for her once again.

That was also the way she dealt with men.

Ted was an old schoolmate; his parents were friends of her parents. Back in the old neighborhood, she began to see him around. She was never all that attracted to him, but he was crazy for her. "He kept coming around," she said as she sat in my office. "I'd say, 'Don't show up tomorrow,' but he would anyway."

On their first date, Ted interrupted her in mid-sentence to walk across the room and kiss her. That may seem romantic for long-time lovers, but on a first date with someone who still hasn't made up her mind about you, that's just rude. And obviously, in his mind, what she was saying was not nearly as important as his romantic agenda. Bonnie was troubled by his behavior, but true to form, she let it pass without comment. She didn't want to create a conflict.

That's how the relationship progressed. Once again, Bonnie was wined and dined and drawn into a relationship. She loved the attention. Yet she knew the man was all wrong for her. He did not share her spiritual interests. Even when he was trying to be good to her, he was overpersistent and rude. He *harassed* her.

When he had her under his spell, the wining and dining degenerated into using and abusing. He would call at the last minute for dates, take her to cheap places, and seem more eager to get physical with her than to talk with her. She found it odd that he never introduced her to his friends, and he often went away for weekends without an explanation. Her friends, her parents, and even her daughter told her to dump him, but she didn't know how.

She tried. Eight times she tried. But he kept coming back, like a bad pizza. He knew how to manipulate her. Again and again, she fell back into his trap: "I keep thinking, *Maybe he'll treat me nice again, like he did at the start.* You forget the bad things. I mean he really treats me like dirt now. But I keep thinking that maybe I did something to make him change."

Ted was the reason Bonnie first came to me. She felt powerless to make a break from him. Even during our sessions, she was erratic. She would be furious with him one week and would defend him the next. Through her counseling, through some journaling, and through our group sessions, she gradually gained perspective and strength. But she used an old strategy to finally break up with him—she moved away. It was just for the summer, but she had an opportunity to work with a Christian ministry in another state. She quickly took it. She knew that from that distance, she would view the relationship more objectively.

Bonnie wrote Ted a stern letter, once and for all ending their romance. He must have sensed how determined she was because he left her alone after that.

About a year later, Bonnie was in her driveway washing her car when Ted drove by. He stopped and honked and waved. She smiled politely and continued washing the car. He stayed there, looking at her, perhaps wondering if she'd come over to talk. She didn't. She was determined to keep him from once again controlling her life. It was a test of wills, and she passed. He had no more power over her.

While Ted seems to have lost his sway over Bonnie, that does not mean her addictive tendencies have disappeared. In fact, she admitted to me that she might still be seeing Ted if she had not gone away for that summer. With continued work, she may be able to overcome these tendencies next time a relationship comes around. But there will be a lot of struggle involved. Her addictive ways are deep-seated; they will not be easy to conquer.

EVALUATION

Bonnie felt inferior as a child. She was constantly seeking her parents' attention. There were no signs of addiction in her family, but perhaps we can trace her addictive tendencies to her longing for love and attention. While this is normal for all children, some seem to have a greater need for attention than others. Some have labeled this love hunger.

When Bonnie married Chris, it seems that she was blinded by her need for love. Chris gave her attention, and she was a sucker for it. She married a man who seemed very giving because of his material generosity, but he turned out to be a big disappointment.

Her second relationship was also a result of her ongoing love hunger. She was afraid of being alone, but added into the formula was the emotional void left by her divorce. She could not risk confronting him about her difficulties with their relationship, so she just moved away. This is her way of solving a problem without really solving it. In a way it works as a cold turkey strategy, and I suppose it's better than staying in an unhealthy relationship. She may have learned this coping method as a child, when she learned how to avoid conflict with her parents. Nothing was ever gained by questioning or arguing. Just agree, or walk away. She's been walking away ever since.

Bonnie's third relationship was also a combination of childhood love hunger and emotional vulnerability. She succumbed to his persistence because her neediness overwhelmed her rational thinking. After a struggle, she broke it off in the usual way, by leaving.

I cannot say that Bonnie is cured, though at present she is free from the bonds of any particular relationship and she is moving forward with her life in a healthier way. She is making her own decisions and working hard to take full responsibility for her future—apart from a man. She has not resolved her excessive need for affirmation. That problem may last a lifetime. But she can learn to live with it and overcome its apparent effects.

Bonnie admits to continued insecurity, saying she would "jump at the chance to be in a relationship." Her lack of personal confidence makes her extremely susceptible to any strong-willed man who comes along. That's why in her more rational moments she reminds herself to be extremely cautious. She has also learned to seek third-party objectivity before moving into anything new.

Others in Bonnie's situation have found that a healthy confrontation once in a while is a big help. I happen to be a conflict avoider, but that quality gets me into more trouble eventually. From this example, we can see that conflict avoiders may try to please others so much that they forfeit their feelings and needs. Breaking these patterns takes commitment and wisdom—the commitment to work at changing natural tendencies and the wisdom to know the proper balance between confrontation and submission.

Bonnie also needs to come to grips with her past. The shock of her bad marriage, a manipulative husband, and an eventual divorce are still with her, especially within her background that tends to demote divorced people to second-class status. Her weakened self-image was further eroded by each new failed relationship. These scars are not quickly healed. Exploration of past hurts, renewed self-confidence, and a belief in a more loving and accepting God have gone a long way toward improving Bonnie's chances for a healthy relationship.

Chapter Nine

BREAKING THE ADDICTIVE CYCLE

Most addiction recovery programs include a step-by-step approach to overcoming problems in your life. There's wisdom in this. Recovery rarely happens quickly or easily. Changes will not happen overnight. It's a process, sometimes long and arduous, but you can take only one step at a time.

The same applies to the relationship addict. The steps of recovery need to be slow, steady changes toward a more balanced understanding of love and toward healthier relationships.

Slow, tiny steps toward recovery were recently humorized in the movie *What About Bob?* A psychiatrist, played by Richard Dreyfuss, advises his client (Bill Murray) on how to overcome his fears and anxieties. He repeatedly tells his client to just take baby steps. At the end of the session, Murray shuffles out of the psychiatrist's office, carefully putting one foot in front of the other, mumbling under his breath, "Baby steps . . . baby steps to the hallway. Now baby steps toward the elevator. Now I'm taking baby steps *onto* the elevator." As the elevator doors begin to close, he yells out, "Hey, this really works. I made it!"

Get that picture in your mind. If you are struggling with an addictive relationship, there is hope for you. Remember that comic mental image of Bill Murray taking his baby steps through life. Step-by-step you can break your addiction. Some steps will seem quite large. But then you'll look back and feel depressed because you still have so far to go. Remember, baby steps; baby steps. If you take one day at a time, you will make progress toward mature, loving relationships.

STEP #1: ADMIT THAT YOU HAVE A PROBLEM AND THAT YOU ARE IN AN ADDICTIVE RELATIONSHIP (OR PRONE TO SUCH RELATIONSHIPS)

Just as the alcoholic begins the AA experience by standing up and announcing, "My name is _____, and I'm an alcoholic," you must first admit your addiction or tendency to yourself and then to others.

That's hard, isn't it? Personal secrets and family secrets can keep us tied up emotionally for years. The secret takes on a special power, reinforced with each new moment of silence. But when we demystify the secret, by saying it out loud and by telling others, it tends to lose some of its power almost immediately.

I see this phenomenon in therapy all the time. People come in with secrets. As they begin to open up, the grip that the information had on their lives is released. And the fact that they are admitting their weaknesses, acknowledging their need for help, is often a major part of the therapeutic battle.

One woman hesitantly told me she had had an abortion. It was a secret known only to her closest friends. She felt terrible about it, but she explained that her circumstances at the time (which included an addictive relationship with a man) had backed her into a corner. And she had lived with awful guilt ever since.

She had a hard time accepting what she had done and felt choked with emotion. But the mere act of confessing it had a powerful effect. A weight had fallen off her back. She had punctured the power of secrecy.

This release is true for many incest survivors. Every day, it seems, we hear a new story of some public figure confronting sexual abuse from childhood. In most cases, the abuses have been shrouded in secrecy for decades, even blocked within the minds of the victims. But when the secret comes out, the past can be dealt with, and a new future unfolds.

In the case of addictions, the secrecy can be even more difficult to overcome. It is a matter of personal weakness; some would call it sin. The addict needs to say, "This thing has a power over me, and I haven't been able to kick it. I have been defeated. I continue to do destructive things." That's hard to say, but it is necessary. It breaks the back of denial.

Denial is the first line of defense for any addiction: "Problem? What problem?" If you pretend it's not a problem, it can go on indefinitely. So when you admit to an addiction or an addictive tendency, you are first of all admitting it *to yourself*. You are facing up to a situation that needs to be corrected. A doctor must diagnose an illness before healing it. This admission is your diagnosis: "I have a problem."

But *publicly* admitting your problem is crucial, too. For one thing, it helps to keep you from slipping back into denial. When I say "publicly," I am referring to disclosure to one or two trusted friends or, at the most, a support group. I am *not* talking about putting an announcement in your community newspaper. Once your friends learn that you have a problem, the secret is out. It's no use hiding it from yourself anymore.

Emotional support is another result of public admission. You can find power in knowing that others have faced or are facing similar problems. People often fear that they will be rejected when they finally let their secrets out. But within the right circle of friends, they frequently find acceptance and love. And that can set in motion a whole system of practical support and accountability.

In my church, one woman explained to her Bible study group how she was mustering up the courage to end a bad relationship.

By the evening's end, one member of that group offered her a place to stay if she needed it, another offered to stay with her, and others offered to be on call if she needed someone to talk to, day or night. She ventured to share her need, and she was met not with rejection but with practical assistance. She also knew that she had become accountable to the people, though they had not pressured her at all. She needed to go ahead with the difficult but necessary breakup.

So the first general step toward healing, if you are in an addictive relationship, is an admission of the nature of that relationship. Admit it to yourself, admit it to your friends, and admit it to the other person in the relationship. If you are not currently in an addictive relationship, but you recognize a tendency in that direction, admit it to yourself and to some close friends. Admitting this tendency will help you to be very careful in entering a new romance.

STEP #2: RECOGNIZE THAT YOU CAN'T CHANGE YOURSELF

Once you've admitted your problem, what do you do about it? Maybe in some cases you could grit your teeth and do what it takes to get whole again and to redeem your relationship. But if you could do that, you probably would have done it by now.

This is the second great lie addicts tell themselves: "I can kick this habit anytime I want." It's the second prong of denial.

In the clear light of day, a woman in an addictive romance may admit, "This is not a healthy relationship." She may even say, "I need to break up with him." But as the sun sets, her old compulsions return. She thinks about him. She needs to see him. She calls him. She goes to see him. And she wakes up the next morning, used, perhaps abused, hating herself. "This is not a healthy relationship," she says. "But I can break up with him anytime I want." Right.

How many of these cycles does it take before you realize that you *can't?* You are held in the power of an addiction that's bigger than you are. You need help.

The Twelve Steps of Alcoholics Anonymous include a reliance on a Higher Power. Many of us call this power God. We have seen how God changes lives. We have seen how people find power in a relationship with God. Countless people have come to our Fresh Start Seminars with deep relational needs and deep spiritual needs as well. Healing happens on both fronts. As they find God, they tap into divine power to restore their relationships.

It's no magic elixir. It's no "get saved and all your problems will go away" kind of thing. But the One who made us has the power to remake us. We can rely on Him for the strength we need to restore our relationships and ourselves.

Skeptics will say that this is just substituting one addiction for another. In fact, they might say that religion is just another form of relationship addiction—only it's a relationship with God.

It is true that religion can be addicting. We can be drawn to the forms and activities in a self-demeaning and self-destructive way. But there's nothing self-destructive about a true relationship with God. He restores us; He builds us up.

As I mentioned in chapter 1, addiction is idolatry. It is a matter of seeking ultimate fulfillment in something or someone that doesn't deliver. We *make* a god out of some substance, activity, or person. Each is a false god, which can never live up to our expectations. As a Christian, I believe that God is the only One who consistently delivers. When God is given top priority, other aspects of life fall into place.

It is no accident that in the first of the Ten Commandments God says, "You shall have no other gods before Me" (Exod. 20:3). When He has that top spot, there is order. Without Him, there is chaos. As our Maker, He takes pleasure in the wholeness of His creation. But when we allow other substances or actions or people to take His place, we are not whole.

The true God goes beyond our expectations. The true God offers us real power to break free of the bonds of false relationships.

So if you are currently struggling to break free from an addictive relationship, look beyond yourself to God. Stop relying on your own power. Ask for His help.

STEP #3: ABANDON THE "DRUG"

Just as the drug addict or alcoholic *must* go cold turkey to un-hook from the drug of choice, so the relationship addict must abandon the relationship along with any hopes of salvaging even a part of it. (This advice applies unless you are in an addictive marriage. There's a special chapter for you later.)

One of the greatest pitfalls that I have observed for relation-ship addicts is their belief that they can maintain a part of the relationship or at least "remain friends." For most people, it might seem only logical, but for the relationship addict, it's di-sastrous. It's just like telling a substance abuser it's okay to drink on weekends or use cocaine on Christmas and his birthday. Ob-viously, that would be ridiculous advice. It would lead only to a relapse.

Relationship addicts often relapse. Why? Because relation-ships are so natural and necessary. It is socially acceptable to be in relationships—and often unacceptable *not* to be in one.

But someone who's just been through a painful breakup doesn't need a new romance. Even if it's not an addictive situa-tion, the postbreakup time requires personal healing, not new love interests. In the case of a relationship addict, the rebound can be devastating.

Many times, people try to end the addictive relationship in a gradual way, "to make it easier for both of us." This rationaliza-tion only prolongs the agony for weeks, months, or even years. Most of the people I've known who tried this method ended up in a limbo relationship that dragged on until *the other person* fi-nally called it quits, which often sent the addict into an absolute tailspin.

We already saw that in Scott's case. His romance with Julie was addictive, and he sensed it. Though they met some needs for each other, there was an unhealthy quality to their interaction.

Scott felt he needed to break it off—but he didn't. He tried but always came back. She would call, "needing" him, and he would scurry back to her.

There came a time when Julie didn't need him anymore. She had grown beyond her traumas and wanted to spread her wings a little, so she broke up with Scott. The experience was devastating for Scott, as you can imagine. The pain struck him physically as well as emotionally.

Yet, even after their final breakup, they were getting together for a time "as friends." She felt guilty about dumping him and wanted to salve his wounds, but she knew she couldn't. Even in the process, they were still flirting with romantic involvement. They were still addicted to each other, though she had established different terms for the relationship.

You may be saying, "Oh, isn't that sweet? It's nice to remain friends with those you've dated." Remaining friends may be acceptable in certain friendships, but it is dangerous for those with unhealthy addictions. Scott was pained and confused during that time. Julie was hurting him in ways she never realized.

I finally suggested to both of them that they avoid each other. It was somewhat difficult since they went to the same church. But I asked them to sit on different sides. They needed a clean break so that the healing could begin.

Don't try to kid yourself. As with any other addiction, an addictive relationship must be stopped *cold turkey!* Immediately! For good! This action is particularly necessary if it is an affair with a married person or if the relationship is destructive to you or your children. End it today!

STEP #4: FIND SUPPORT AND ACCOUNTABILITY

Let's say you have mustered the strength to end the relationship. It took all you had, but you did it, and now you're free. Congratulations!

But what happens a few hours later when the adrenaline subsides? When you eat dinner alone or go to a movie alone? Instinctively, you reach for that person you've grown accustomed to. That person isn't there. You begin to feel an emptiness inside.

Do you reach for the phone, call your former lover, and patch things up? No, you mustn't. Once again, you grab the strength you need, and you withstand that temptation.

A few days pass. People ask about your "better half." That's how you feel. Half. You explain things to your closest friends and let the others draw their own conclusions.

You get to the weekend. No dates. Munching popcorn in front of the TV, you remember the joys of weekends past with your ex-lover. Somehow the bad times have vanished from your memory. "Maybe my ex would still take me back," you muse.

It's your birthday. Or maybe your ex's birthday. Or Christmas. A special time, and you're alone again. How will you ever get through? Day after day you fight the urge to run back, to turn back the clock, to climb back into that old relationship. That emptiness still gnaws at you.

And what happens, sometime during that torturous process, when your ex-lover calls you? "Let's get together and talk . . . just as friends. We need to talk." You're a pushover. The trapdoor opens. You fall through.

In the wake of a breakup, the pressure to get back together is enormous. It can build through the first few hours of the breakup to a mighty crescendo of emotional despair over the next several months. I have found few who could survive withdrawal on their own.

What was missing from the scenario I just presented? A support group. Or at least an individual friend who could hold you accountable to your decision. You need a sponsor, as many in the recovery movement refer to it. The person or group of people must have regular contact with you and must not accept your first response to "How are you doing?" The sponsor must be willing to probe well beneath the surface.

The right group of friends can fill some of the emptiness inside you. They can eat popcorn with you on Saturday nights.

And they can monitor your emotions. When you are in danger of slipping back, they can warn you. They will never be able to make your decisions for you, but they can help you clarify the situation.

Friends can remind you of the bad times. As you look back on an addictive relationship, you tend to remember only the highs. The lows disappear. Friends are there to tell you what a jerk the other person was, how miserable you were, and how lucky you are to be free.

Addictive relationships tend to exclude other friends. A jealous lover may force you to dissolve old friendships, or you may be so enthralled with your lover that you forget about everyone else. The problem is, these are the very times when you need a circle of close friends. They help you keep your perspective. If your lover is crossing your boundaries, your friends can tell you. They also help you keep a sense of "you." You remain a well-rounded person because you are not totally consumed by your lover.

If you already have a circle of friends to do these things for you, great! But perhaps you have alienated old friends and failed to make new ones. You may need to build new friendships, perhaps among your family or casual acquaintances, or restore old ones. If nothing else, consult a pastor or church leader who can put you in touch with caring Christians. Or find a counselor who can connect you with an area support group. Much like AA groups, sex and love addiction groups have formed all across the country. It may be a "manufactured" support system, but it may grow into genuine friendship.

In any case, you need to *empower* your friends to support you. That is, you must tell them if you want them to check up on you. One unwritten rule in this society is "live and let live." Many people will consider it rude to pry too deeply into your business—unless you ask them to. If you need their support, say so. If you need their advice, ask for it. If you need their warnings and challenges and scoldings, let them know.

You'll probably need all of the above.

STEP #5: KEEP A JOURNAL OF YOUR FEELINGS AND PROGRESS

If you don't have friends to remind you of the bad old days, you can do this for yourself by keeping a journal. This exercise is especially helpful if you are in the middle of an addictive relationship. Start now. Record the good and the bad experiences. Record how you feel each day. Be brutally honest with yourself.

Then from time to time as you struggle with the relationship, go back and reread the journal. It will give you a sense of your relational history.

Are you having the same struggles you had a year or two ago? Are you making the same promises to yourself? ("If she doesn't shape up in three months, I'm out of here!") If so, that should tell you something. You're stuck.

Or have you sunk deeper into an unhealthy relationship? Are you more attached to the other person than you used to be? Are you more dependent? How has the relationship been unhealthy for you over the years? As you read your journal again, do you like what you're reading? Are you flattered by the picture it gives of you, the writer? Or do you see poor priorities, twisted logic, and a weak will?

Idealization is a major problem I see again and again with people I counsel. It's the old rose-colored glasses routine. I usually ask such people to go back and read out loud from their journals. It's usually a poignant testimony about a troubled relationship—sleepless nights, neglect, abuse. After only a few pages, the reality of the destructiveness of the relationship comes crashing back again.

If you are in an unhealthy relationship, journaling can be a way of recording your reasons for getting out of it. You can use this information not to attack the other person but to bolster you in your resolve to get free. If you have already broken free, go back and find the journaling you may have done earlier. Remember how it *really* was.

STEP #6: UNDERSTAND YOUR ADDICTIVE CYCLE, AND LEARN TO CONTROL IT

Most people have a point of no return, that is, a point at which all reason goes out the window and they decide to go with their emotions. For the relationship addict, that point is dangerous. Picture yourself at the top of a steep hill and you're wearing roller skates. As you skate around the hilltop, you have some control over your motion, but when you go too far over the edge—well, it's downhill from there.

If you are a relationship addict, if you have a tendency toward unhealthy relationships, you must learn where your point of no return is. And while you're still on top of the hill, establish good habits and make wise decisions (take off those skates!). Don't wait until you're in your descent.

The alcoholic learns that he can't go into a bar. He knows that he can't take the temptation, so he avoids it entirely. The drug addict learns that she can't hang around with the old crowd. They would start pulling her down that slope.

In the same way, the relationship addict needs to learn the triggers for those old dysfunctional patterns of relating. These triggers may include

- holidays, birthdays, or special anniversary dates.
- an introduction to someone new with whom you fall head over heels in love almost immediately.
- your idea that someone *really needs you.*
- the feeling of being undervalued at your job or with your family.
- a major loss or crisis.
- the feeling of loneliness or depression.

You must recognize these dangerous situations and guard your decisions accordingly. Your emotions must be on red alert at these times. Do not make rash commitments. Think things through. Get feedback from others.

Besides finding your trigger points, you need to find some

safe havens. Get a group of friends together, or meet with one or two friends who are on call for you. Maybe there's an activity you can sink yourself into for a while or just a way of talking yourself through the crisis. On more serious occasions, you could consult a pastor or counselor.

The idea is *preventive maintenance*. Be aware of your red-flag times, and do what you need to do to get through them.

STEP #7: EXAMINE YOUR SELF-WORTH AND IDENTITY

Where do you find fulfillment? What makes you feel most like yourself? When do you feel important? Who are you really?

These questions strike at the root of the sense of self. And that is precisely where most of us get into trouble with addictive relationships. I grab on to someone else because I need to feel fulfilled. For some romance addicts, it doesn't matter who it is; they just need *someone* to be in love with. For some sex addicts, it doesn't matter, either; they just need someone to have a sexual encounter with. If they aren't in a relationship—romantic or sexual—they just aren't themselves.

A friend called me and told me about her new boyfriend. She was bothered because she was clinging desperately to him, terrified that he would leave her. My friend was a professional actress, finding it hard to get work. The romance was the highlight of her life, and she didn't want to let go of it.

Always the counselor, I asked her many questions about the relationship and about her life. She was full of praise for her boyfriend and full of complaints about her other friends, her family, and her attempts to get work. "When you're with him, you feel like you're worth something," I suggested. "And when you're not with him, you feel like garbage. Right?"

"Exactly," she said, her voice showing amazement. "How did you know?"

Talk to relationship addicts long enough and you hear patterns in their speech that betray certain ways of thinking. You hear comments like these:

- "I just couldn't live without her."
- "He makes me feel like I'm somebody."
- "When I'm with her, I don't care what anyone else says."
- "When I'm with him, I don't have to worry about anything."
- "Before I met her, I was a mess."
- "Who am I? I'm John's wife."

There's nothing wrong with these statements per se. But listen to them carefully, and you'll hear some underlying problems. The one who "couldn't live" without his girlfriend implies that he has no life of his own. It's great if he makes you feel like "somebody," but would you be somebody if he weren't around? Of course you would! It may be a nice romantic fantasy to forget about the rest of the world when you're with that special someone, but you are still a member of the human race with all the accompanying responsibilities. It may be true that your lover pulled you out of a "mess," but does that mean your life will always be a mess without this person? Yes, you are John's wife, but you are much, much more.

In general, people in addictive relationships don't like themselves very much. They long for someone to take them out of themselves or somehow to fulfill them, save them, or make them worthy. If you are in an addictive relationship or have that tendency, you probably know what I'm talking about. You're seeking either to prove yourself or to lose yourself. Neither is very healthy.

Recovery requires that you first *examine your assumptions about yourself*. You may already know that you have a poor self-image—or you may be surprised to discover that fact. David, from our original group, thought he had a great self-image. But as he examined his assumptions, he realized that he had always felt inadequate with women. His addiction to the conquest of women stemmed from that inadequacy; he kept trying to prove himself worthy. There are many overachieving women, strong and confident in the workplace, who subconsciously see every romance as a way of proving themselves to distant or alcoholic fathers.

What do you really think of yourself? That's a crucial question to consider.

Once you're in touch with your self-image, what do you do? *Get real*. Seriously, take a realistic look at yourself—apart from any relationship you're in. What kind of person are you? Are you really as inadequate as you fear? What are your strong points? What people find you valuable, and why? What does God think of you? Consult friends, counselors, or church leaders to get their opinions.

Then *talk to yourself*. You may think the self-talk idea is corny, but it works. Tell yourself that you are important, that you are a valuable person, even enjoyable. Learn to like yourself. Praise yourself when you do something well. (And hang around others who praise you rather than put you down.) If nothing else, find a simple phrase to repeat to yourself when you begin to doubt your worth, something like "I am created by God and loved by God and others. I am worth something."

If you become more satisfied with yourself, you will not need to seek your identity in someone else.

STEP #8: SEE A COUNSELOR

If the addictive cycle continues to be a problem for you, seek more intensive counseling with a therapist who can help you understand your addictive patterns and overcome them.

Counseling is not just for people with mental disorders. In some ways all of us can benefit from counseling, especially if we find healthy relationships elusive. All of us have certain blind spots about our behavior and attitudes. Counseling will not solve all of your problems, but it is designed to give you insights into why you behave the way you do and suggest steps you can take to overcome some of your unhealthy patterns.

Counseling provides a sounding board and another layer of accountability. It sometimes helps to have someone to answer to—and a professional authority figure at that.

The general guidelines of these eight steps will help you break free of addictive relationships and/or stay free of them. The next chapter presents more specific recommendations for people at various points of the addictive cycle.

_____ *Chapter Ten* _____

THE CANYON

A group of children went on a field trip to a national park in the mountains. For safety's sake (or so they thought), each child had a partner, so no one would be lost. A rope was looped around each partner's waist with an arm's length of rope between them.

They went to one particularly scenic canyon and stood on the edge, peering down at the stream below. "Be careful, children!" the teacher shouted. "Don't go too close to the edge." Of course, several children immediately went too close to the edge. There they began to play, spinning around, winding themselves up in the rope.

Annie and Barry lost their footing. They began to slide down the edge of the canyon. Luckily, they grabbed some rocks and stopped their descent just a few yards down. The teacher hurried to the scene and carefully coached them: "Stay calm. Don't move suddenly. Try to get untangled from the rope. Good. Now, Barry, help Annie get over to that rock on your right. Good. Now, Annie, pull Barry over with you."

In fifteen painstaking minutes, the children climbed back and

115

were pulled to safety. But a few pairs of kids were oblivious to those events. They were a stone's throw away, doing the same shenanigans that had gotten Annie and Barry in their mess. Cindy and Dan got so wrapped up that they could not move their arms.

"Look, I'm a mummy!" yelled Cindy, her skinny arms tight to her sides.

"Then I'm the daddy!" yelled Dan, bound next to her.

Evie tugged at her rope. "Come on, Frank. Let's do what they're doing!"

Frank hesitated. "I suppose if they jump into a lake, we have to do that, too." But tossing her curly blonde hair, Evie was already winding herself up in the rope and circling Frank.

In their revelry, they hardly noticed the rocks at their feet giving way. All four plummeted into the canyon, helpless to do anything. They got to the bottom, bruised but alive. They cried. They yelled at each other. They worried about what might happen.

"I can't move," said Dan.

"Why not?" Cindy asked, frightened. "Are you paralyzed?"

"No, I think it's just the rope."

"Maybe we could unwind it."

"I don't know," Dan answered. "That seems like an awful lot of work."

Evie and Frank had fallen a short distance away from the other pair. They, too, discovered that the rope was hindering their movement.

"Let's get untangled, Evie. It'll be dark soon, and I heard there are bears around here."

"Do you always believe everything you hear?" Evie taunted.

"Everything except what you tell me," Frank retorted. "No, it's true. A park ranger told me."

"Oh."

"You got us into this, Evie," Frank said sternly, tugging at the ropes. "Now help me get us out."

"Can't we keep the rope on?" Evie wondered. "You're just going to run away and leave me for the bears."

"It would serve you right."

By now, the teacher had a bullhorn and was calling to the fallen children. "We are sending help, children, but it's getting dark. You must help us help you. First, you have to unwind the ropes. Then you'll be able to move freely. You have to climb out the other side of the canyon. It's not as steep there, and signs mark the trail. The park rangers will meet you on the other side. Go quickly, children, while there's still light!"

"I'm afraid," said Dan.

"So am I," Cindy responded.

"I don't think we can get out of these ropes, Cindy. Maybe we can just crawl back up the hill together."

"But the teacher said to go the other way."

"Yeah, but we're right here. Look, it's closer this way. Maybe we can climb back up."

"Okay, let's try it."

They struggled together and moved a few feet. It was too tiring, especially with their bruises. They stopped.

"We'll never get out," Dan whimpered "We'll just be eaten by the alligators."

"Alligators?" asked Cindy.

Meanwhile, Frank was furiously trying to extricate himself from the rope. Furiously, indeed, since Evie was doing everything she could to thwart him.

"Don't leave me!" she whined.

"I don't want to leave you, Evie!" he barked. "But we can't go anywhere like this. It's best for us both if we get untangled."

"No! You're going to run away and leave me for the bears."

"I'm sure you can manage, Goldilocks."

The teacher periodically called instructions from above. "See that tall pine tree just across the stream? Head for that. The stream is shallow there, and that's where the trail is. Move quickly, children. It's getting dark!"

Every few minutes, Dan and Cindy would struggle a few more feet, but they weren't getting far. And they refused to undo the rope.

Frank, on the other hand, succeeded in getting untangled. But Evie was being obstinate.

"Will you move your arm, stupid, so I can get this rope off you?"

"Don't call me that."

"What? Stupid? Well, then, don't be so stupid and I won't call you that."

"I'm not being stupid. I just don't want you to run away."

"I'm not running away, Evie. Look, I'm untangling your rope. Does this look like I'm running away?"

"You're just trying to be nice. But when I'm untangled, then you'll run away."

"And you can run with me."

"I'm not as fast as you."

"I'll run slower."

"You will not. Boys never run slow."

"I will, Evie, I promise."

"Will not."

"Will you just move your stupid arm?"

"My arm is not stupid!"

Frank stopped and glared at his partner. "It's going to be broken if you don't move it."

Evie moved her arm. Frank pulled the rope around her and found another snag.

"Now lift your foot, Evie."

"You don't like me, do you?"

"Sure I like you. Lift your foot."

"You'd rather be tied up with Marcie, wouldn't you?"

"Marcie would be lifting her foot right now."

"I knew you liked her. That's why you're leaving me to the bears."

Frank stopped again and wiped his young forehead with his wrist. "To be honest, Evie, I don't think the bears would want you."

"I knew it. You hate me. You're going to run away."

Frank handed Evie the portion of rope he had untangled. "Here, you try it. I'm going to run and get help. I'll send them back for you."

"I knew it."

He darted off toward the tall tree across the stream. As he went, he heard Evie's plaintive voice crying, "Here I am, bears! Come and get me!"

Frank's ascent was difficult. He slipped while fording the stream and got all wet, but he reached the tree and saw the signs marking the trail. He had to stop several times on the climb. When he did, he heard occasional wails from Evie in the canyon below. He thought about going back to her. Even if he did reach the top, the rangers would never get to her before dark. And if there really were bears . . .

Once he even turned around and headed back toward Evie, but then he remembered their argument. Even if he did go back, he figured, he would never get her untangled. So he plodded up the hill again.

Soon he heard voices. Rangers. He called out and they answered. Around the bend and they were there, their flashlights dancing in the darkening wood. Frank told them where he had left Evie and where he thought Cindy and Dan had fallen, and several rangers rushed downward while one carried him up the hill.

You can make up your own ending to this story. Frank made it to safety by untangling himself. Were the others eaten by bears or alligators? You make the call.

ADDICTION CANYON

We have talked about addiction as a cycle, something that's repeated again and again, with tragic results in the lives of its victims. Relationship addiction can also be viewed as a dangerous canyon. You can stand at the crest, teeter on the edge, plummet down the side, wallow at the bottom, or climb out the other side.

This image helps us as we talk about recovery. The solutions are different for those on different spots in this canyon. In the early stages of relationship addiction, you can still retreat. You can come back to the top of the hill where the footing is safer. It is possible that some relationships teetering on the edge of addiction can be saved. Annie and Barry, in the parable just told, are the picture of this situation. They had not fallen far. They were able to edge back to safety.

But once you're in, once you've fallen into the canyon, the only way out is up the other side. There was no way Cindy and Dan could climb back up the steep slope they had fallen down. Recovery, at this point, requires that you ditch the relationship and find personal healing on your own. Frank could have argued with Evie all night, but it wouldn't have helped either of them. His disentanglement brought the possibility of deliverance for both of them.

The road to wholeness is not easy. The way out of Addiction Canyon is steep and tedious, but step-by-step you can make it— if you don't look back.

Obviously, that's the most difficult thing about an addictive relationship—breaking up. People keep wondering, "Can't we just do things to make it less addictive? Can't we stay together and give each other more space?" The answer is no if the relationship is deeply addictive. There is no climbing back up that slope once you've hit bottom.

I need to mention one exception to this rule: marriage. I do not recommend that partners in addictive marriages ditch the relationship and go it alone. They have the tremendous task of restoring the health of their relationship, honoring their marriage vows. (Chapter 16 discusses this subject in detail.)

Let me go on and prescribe specific courses of action for people at different points in Addiction Canyon. (See fig. 1.) I will be taking the general steps of the last chapter and applying them to specific situations.

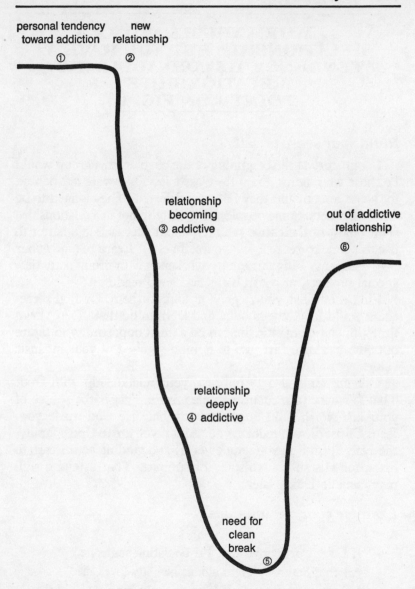

FIGURE 1. Points sliding into and climbing
out of Addiction Canyon.

1. WHEN YOU'RE NOT IN A RELATIONSHIP, BUT YOU HAVE A TENDENCY TOWARD ADDICTIVE RELATIONSHIPS (POINT 1 ON FIG. 1)

Build your sense of self

In our story at the beginning of the chapter, this group would be those who didn't go on the class trip. They were left behind for some reason, and they felt very dejected. They longed to be with the others. Some people, when they're not in a relationship, spend most of their time whining about that fact. It's better to use this time to get to know yourself better. Learn to enjoy your own company. Fill your empty weekends with group activities, special projects, or warm baths and good reading.

Find the things you're good at and do them. Or find something you'd like to be good at and learn to do that. The "down time" in your romantic life can be a great opportunity to figure out who you really are and to remind yourself of your intrinsic value.

Use this time also to improve your relationship with God. That is where your identity comes from. That is the source of your self-worth. You are somebody because God made you. Jesus Christ died to redeem you. And if you are in God's family, the Holy Spirit is in you, empowering and guiding you. Learn to listen for His subtle whispers of support. That listening skill may come in handy later.

Examine your assumptions

- "If I was worth anything, I'd be dating someone."
- "Another Saturday night alone. Nobody loves me."
- "I have so much to offer! If no one asks me out, all of that goes to waste!"
- "Look at her—one boyfriend after another. She is so lucky!"

- "What a babe! Life would be so great if she were my girlfriend!"
- "Friendship is nice, but if he really cared about me, he'd be asking me out."

All of these assumptions are faulty. But they're common among people who aren't in romantic relationships. Our society attaches gargantuan importance to dating and marriage and sexual relationships. The assumptions listed above are reinforced by the media and in everyday conversations. We assume that those who are "with someone" are happy, and those who aren't, aren't.

Take a close look at your assumptions. When you start to say something about the value of being with someone else (or the tragedy of being alone), stop yourself and think about it first. Faulty assumptions lead to faulty decisions.

See the wholeness in yourself and others

Relationship addiction often arises from a feeling of emptiness. "If only I were attached to that person," you say, "I would be complete." That's nonsense, of course, but that's the prevailing attitude. And when you say that, you're doing two unhealthy things: you're demeaning yourself, and you're demeaning the other person.

First of all, you are ignoring the fact that you are a valuable person in your own right, complete within yourself. By relying on the other person for wholeness, you are putting pressure on the relationship and abdicating your responsibility for yourself.

Second, you are defining the other person as a need-meeter. That person has value to you *only as the person meets your needs*. You may "need" someone to be with on Saturday nights or someone to parade before your friends. You may "need" someone to put you through med school or someone to provide you with children. You may "need" someone to share the bills with, to balance the checkbook, or to give you backrubs. But as soon as you begin to define that person by how the person meets your need, you're in trouble.

Men who are battling sex addiction view women as objects for their lust. Women are reduced to pretty faces and shapely bodies; they are not seen as whole people. (Increasingly, women are viewing men this way, too.) Love addicts may conjure fantasies based on one small detail about a person. They think they are loving that person, but they are worshiping an image based on merely part of that person.

Fight this. Work to see the wholeness in everyone you meet. When you see people with pretty faces or shapely bodies, ask about their families or any good books they've read lately. Find their flaws and accept them. See them as complete people, even as you remind yourself of your wholeness.

2. WHEN YOU'RE BEGINNING A NEW RELATIONSHIP, AND YOU RECOGNIZE THAT YOU HAVE A GENERAL TENDENCY TOWARD ADDICTIVE RELATIONSHIPS (POINT 2 ON FIG. 1)

Go slow

Let the relationship grow slowly. It's not a bad idea to set limits on how often you see your new love interest or talk on the phone—no more than one date a week and a limit of two phone calls. Some have suggested dating several people casually at the same time, though this, too, can create problems.

The early stages of a relationship set patterns that will be followed throughout the relationship. People with addictive tendencies tend to rush headlong into new romances, creating unhealthy patterns of relating. Many potentially good relationships are sabotaged because the participants rushed things at the start and never knew how to cool down. You need to keep your balance. Don't lose yourself.

The students in our story were tied together and played around oblivious to the danger they were in. Look down, see the pit, and notice that the rocks you are standing on are loose. Go slow. Walk carefully. And continually remind your partner of the dangers below.

Hold off on the physical

Sex has power all its own. Intended as an expression of whole-person intimacy (and ultimately expressed within marriage), sexual activity can quickly defy those intentions and become the main event. Sex is a crooked politician, making wild promises just to get elected. Sex is a dark cloud hanging over the guilt ridden. Sex is a weapon that frequently backfires. But within a healthy marriage, sex is a treasure.

You meet someone you're very attracted to. You begin the conquest. You do all the things that lead to a solid relationship, and things are going well. Then one fine night you get sexually involved with the person. And that changes everything. You have completed the conquest, and now you're not so interested.

Or maybe you're still interested, but your interest begins to focus on sex. Now the most important thing is how the person makes you feel sexually. The relationship is cheapened. You find it practically impossible to go on a date without ending up in bed.

You believe in saving sexual intercourse for marriage. But this new relationship is so intense, you go too far. Now you feel bound to this person. You have shared special intimacies. Maybe if you stay with this person, it will all be okay. The relationship crumbles around you, but you desperately hold on. You end up clinging to an unhealthy situation because you can't forgive yourself and start over.

Can you relate to any of these scenarios? They occur when people rush into physical interaction. Relationships quickly go out of balance, especially when you have addictive tendencies to start with. Obviously, there is a wide range from holding hands to having sexual intercourse. I'm not going to give you a scorecard, just a strong caution: hold back; be careful; go slow; be strong. The health of this new relationship depends on it.

Set aside some self-time

I already talked about limiting the frequency of your dates. This is the flip side of that strategy. One problem in addictive relationships is that people *lose themselves*. They spend every waking hour (and some sleeping hours) with, planning to be with, thinking about, or dreaming about the object of their affection. They are consumed. They see themselves only as an adjunct to the other person, some sort of sidecar.

It is essential that you take time to nourish yourself, to get in touch with yourself, to remember who you are, apart from the other person. Establish this habit early in your relationship and it will strengthen you throughout. Set aside a special time—fifteen minutes a day, two hours a week, or every Saturday morning or Sunday evening—as *your* time. This is time to be alone with yourself (or with God) and get grounded again.

Keep your friends

Do not let your lover decide who your friends will be. Sometimes this is done flagrantly as a jealous lover resents the time you spend with longtime pals. It can also be done subtly as your lover gently discourages those other friendships or plans events so that you'll have to break dates with your friends. It can also be done by you as you get so wrapped up in your new lover that you let old friendships slide.

Don't let it happen. First, let your partner know that your friendships are special to you and *will* continue to be (though you may have to assure your partner that there's no romantic threat).

Second, confront any subtle manipulation on the part of your lover and bring it out into the open: "I know you don't like Bill and Judy, but I've promised to have dinner with them this week. I'm not asking you to come, but I can't break that date to be with you. I'm sorry. It's not that they're more important to me than you are, but I do want to keep them as friends, and I do want to keep my promises."

Third, combat your tendencies to neglect your friends. Work at restoring valuable friendships that may be slipping away.

Trust your friends' opinions

Your friends know you. They may know some of your romantic history. If you are entering a new romance, you probably have some blind spots. You need the opinions of those who know you best. They are not always right, but their opinions, combined with your own, are valuable.

You may need to seek out their opinions. Sometimes friends will not venture to pry into your business. But if you ask them, they may provide some helpful cautions.

Communicate fully from the start

Misunderstandings that take root in the early days of a relationship can grow into conflicts that create great pain: "But I thought . . ."; "But you said . . ." Years later you find yourself bound to a person you don't really know.

Early in a relationship, you want to assume that everything will be fine. You are looking through those rose-colored glasses and excusing all sorts of things: "Three hours late for a date? That's fine. I needed to catch up on my macrame." As a result, you don't establish the boundary lines that need to be set up. You can walk all over each other and never know it.

- "I don't want him to think that I'm . . . a nag, a prude, a whiner, unfeeling, unsophisticated."
- "I don't want her to think that I'm . . . a jerk, a prude, ignorant, poor, unconfident, unmasculine."

You know what this is like, don't you? You do the dance, presenting false images of yourself and assuming the best about the other. (I heard a comic say, "I hate dates. You spend the whole night trying to pretend you're something you're not, hoping to get her to the point where she'll accept you for who you are.") Reality crashes in later, often with destructive results.

Be honest from the outset. Try to present yourself honestly and perceive the other person with the same honesty. Talk through the conflicts, even if they seem minor. If you can learn to work through the minor differences, you've gone a long way toward establishing a healthy relationship. Consider this response: "You were three hours late, and that really bothered me. It made me feel that you really don't care about me, and maybe that's true. I think you're worth another chance, but don't be late, and if you are late, you need to call. I deserve better treatment than what you just gave me." Look! Boundaries, emotional disclosure, and self-esteem are evident. If you can say all that (and if it's accepted), there's hope for the relationship.

3. WHEN YOU'RE IN A RELATIONSHIP THAT'S BECOMING ADDICTIVE (POINT 3 ON FIG. 1)

So you're in this relationship. After maybe three or four months of dating, the two of you have grown together. Your dates and conversations are frequent and exclusive. Your worlds are beginning to revolve around each other. But something is vaguely bothersome.

Then you read a book like this one. And you define some of the danger zones. "Yeah, that's us," you say. "I *am* losing myself. This relationship *is* built on need."

What do you do?

Or maybe you've been in the relationship a long time, but it's been changing recently. A crisis has changed you or the other person. Perhaps an addiction of some kind has surfaced. Whatever, you begin to notice these addictive symptoms in your relationship.

What do you do?

You're on the slope but not far down it. The problems have begun to appear, but they're not deep-seated. This is the region of no easy answers. Can the relationship be saved? Maybe. Maybe not.

Just like Annie and Barry, you've lost your footing, but you may be able to climb back out together. They helped each other, almost leapfrogging their way back up the slope. If you are determined to have a healthy relationship, sometimes you can pull each other back to a safer spot. Here are some steps you might consider:

Evaluate the relationship—and the danger

Does this relationship have the potential of being healthy? Is the relationship so good that it has to be saved? This is a catch-22 question, along the lines of "Are you a compulsive liar?" If you are addicted, you'll say, "Yes, yes, this relationship is the best thing that's ever happened to me!"—even if it isn't. You may need to rely on opinions from friends and family.

Does the other person strengthen you? The question is *not,* Does the other person make up for your mistakes? or Does the other person make you feel better? or Does the other person meet your needs? It is, Does the other person *make you stronger?* It's the difference between being an *enabler* (in the modern recovery parlance) and an *empowerer.* An enabler merely allows you to continue functioning in a dependent way. An empowerer helps you toward independence and interdependence.

If this person were taken away from you, you would be hurt. But would you be at a total loss? Or would you be able to function on your own?

Your relationship may have some addictive elements, but if true empowering is going on, there is hope for it.

How important is the relationship to you? When you look at this romance in the clear light of day, is it something you want to sink your life into? Is it something you want to put a lot of work into? Or is it filling a temporary need in your life? If the relationship is not worth all that much to you, get out. That is, if you sense that it's becoming addictive, get out while you still can. It will get harder and harder to do that.

What practical considerations apply? How interwoven is your life with your lover's life? *Can* you get out now? In the case of marriage, there's a whole different set of rules. You *have* to try to make that work. But perhaps you're dating a coworker or a neighbor. The proximity of these people can create extra ropes to bind you into the relationship trap, much like the kids in the story—at the edge of the cliff and all tangled up with each other. You need to be aware of these practical constraints and do what you can to remain unsnared.

If you decide to end the relationship, move on to situations 4 and 5. Since the addiction is just beginning, it will not be as serious as the cases of those who are well entrenched, but the same principles apply.

If you think it's best to stay in the relationship and to try to make it less addictive, read on.

Agree together to change things

It takes two to tangle and to untangle. Talk together about the addictive nature of your relationship. Discuss how you want things to be between you, a healthy love in which both partners are honored. If your partner does not agree to work through this with you, your chances of restoration are slim to none.

Consider taking a vacation from each other

Yes, such "vacations" are often the prelude to a breakup. But they can also provide valuable rebuilding time for the individuals involved. In an addictive relationship, you need to restore and protect your sense of self, apart from the other person. Set aside a couple of weeks to a month when you will not see each other or have any contact (or maybe just by phone). You will probably learn a lot about yourself and the relationship. You may find that you're better off without the other person. Or you may come back together that much stronger.

Stop the physical relationship

At least for a time, set stark new boundaries on your physical interaction. Say, "For the next month, let's try just kissing good night at the door."

This guideline is about discipline. Consider it an experiment or a corrective procedure. You will be terribly frustrated if you are used to sexual intimacy. But your relationship should be rebalanced.

Sex throws things out of balance. The "intimacy" it provides is shallow, often need oriented, and one-sided. When sexual intimacy is not supported by whole-person commitment, it can contribute to an addiction.

Calling a moratorium, even a temporary one, on the sexual interaction can help the other aspects of the relationship to catch up. You can discover whole new aspects of the other person. On the other hand, if you are *unable* to be nonphysical for even a month, how healthy is that relationship?

Build or rebuild outside friendships

As I said before, addictive relationships can destroy other friendships. You zero in on your lover, and no one else matters. You can put the brakes to this by making a point to maintain your friendships or make new friends. You may have already alienated some old friends. Try to win them back. Ask forgiveness, and express how much you need them at this time (and promise to be there for them as well).

Create personal projects for yourself

To keep from losing yourself in the relationship, set aside time to be by yourself. Or consider taking on a new self-building project. Join a theater group or take piano lessons or tutor inner-city kids. Do this on your own; do not involve your partner. A partner who resists your attempts at self-building exerts too much control over you. You need to grow so that you can be a fuller person as well as a whole partner in the relationship. If your partner can't accept that, you need to jump ship.

Keep a journal

Journaling has numerous benefits. It gets you in touch with your feelings, and it also serves as a record that you can consult later when your memory plays tricks on you.

4. WHEN YOU'RE IN A RELATIONSHIP THAT'S DEEPLY ADDICTIVE (POINT 4 ON FIG. 1)

You're farther down the slope. You are solidly in the relationship and solidly addicted to it. Your life is about this other person. You have forgotten who you are—you think of yourself only in relation to your partner. What can you do to save this relationship, to make it healthy again?

Nothing.

Like the kids in the story that began this chapter, you must untangle the rope and run out the other side. You cannot climb back up the slope. The relationship is doomed. Cindy and Dan tried to climb out of the pit together but found they were too entangled and were going out the wrong way.

What do you need to do for yourself? Get out of the relationship as quickly and cleanly as you can. In this regard, Frank was the only one who had the right idea. He sought to free himself from Evie and to run for help on his own.

It will not be easy. It's like the drug abuser quitting drugs cold turkey. You have to decide to do it and then do what you've decided. All sorts of forces will compel you to stay in the relationship, not the least of which is your partner. But you must be strong and get out. You will not find personal healing until you do.

Now *how* do you accomplish this huge deed?

Decide to do it

It almost goes without saying, but you need to make up your mind that you are going to break off the relationship. And not because this book tells you to, not because anyone else decides it's best. You need to decide for yourself. (You may want to go back and review chapter 9 again and apply those principles.)

Know why you're doing it

What reasons do you have? How is the relationship unhealthy for you? Make a list so you're clear about this. This list is not for anyone else, just for you. You do not need to convince your partner that these reasons are valid; you need to convince yourself. If you waver, go back to the list. (Previous journaling will help, too.)

Build your strength and self-esteem

This step might actually be first. If you know you need to break up, but you don't think you can, go on a self-building campaign. Tell yourself good things about yourself. Hang around people who like you and show it. Addictive relationships tend to knock down your self-esteem, and that saps your strength. Building yourself up will put you in position to make this difficult break.

Decide when and where and how you will make the break

Be specific. Don't make vague promises to yourself. Say, "Monday at lunch, we'll talk, and I'll do it."

Rely on your friends for moral support and accountability

Let them remind you why you're breaking up. Let them encourage you. Don't be afraid to ask them for encouragement. Let a few close friends know when you are planning to break up, and ask them to hold you accountable. You have to go through with it then, or you will be letting them down.

Don't be afraid to cause a scene, look foolish, or cause pain

No one wants to be the bad guy. Not one of us wants to hurt someone we care about. But this is something that has to be done, and there's no nice way to do it. Your partner may cry or yell or say hateful things. Be prepared for all of that and steel yourself to it. There is probably no gentle way to do this.

Think of yourself as a parent taking a child to the doctor for a much-needed shot. It will hurt. And the parent hates the child's pain as much as the child does. But it must be done. No matter how much the child whimpers and whines, the loving parent will go through with it. It is far better for the child in the long run to endure the pain and accept the shot's healing power. You are administering a necessary shot that will be best for you and your partner.

You may want to choose a public location for the breakup conversation to prevent your partner from attacking or seducing you. (People can "fight back" in either way.) You may want to leave yourself an out, such as paying for lunch beforehand so you can leave if things get too heated. Do not respond to a partner's threat to cause a scene in a public place. It may be embarrassing for the moment, but it's not worth undoing the good thing you've done.

Don't give it "one more chance"

You've made your decision. Stick with it. There have probably been numerous "one more chances" before. Don't buy it. You may feel that you're being unreasonable, but don't worry about being unreasonable. You need to hold to your decision. Beware of new evidence your partner may bring in to try to keep you. By this, I mean something new, maybe even surprising, that your partner has never done or said before—making promises, maybe proposing marriage. Sensing that you're serious, your partner may do all sorts of things to change your mind, to get you thinking, *Maybe it will be different this time.*

It won't be different. Go through with the breakup. If those promises have any validity, you'll have to examine them later, much later, when you're free from the addictive trap. Right now, don't let anything diminish your resolve.

After the breakup, avoid the other person

You cannot "just be friends." That seems like the civilized thing to do, but it is far too risky. You will likely be pulled right back into the addiction. The "just friends" line is something you may want to say during the breakup conversation to ease the pain, but it doesn't work in real life.

You may have to take bold action. If you're working with the person, you may need to request a transfer or change jobs. (I realize that's easier said than done, but your emotional health might require it.) If you live near the person, you may need to move or at least change your normal route so you don't run into the person. If you go to church with the person, you may need to make a speical effort to stay away from classes that person attends, for instance, or you may need to visit a different church for a while.

5. WHEN YOU FEEL IT'S IMPOSSIBLE TO GO COLD TURKEY (POINT 5 ON FIG. 1)

When you're in the very bottom of the pit, you feel as if you can't make it. You are tempted to give up because after all, "Isn't a bad relationship better than no relationship at all?" No, it's not. But I know it can be hard to convince yourself of that.

Try anyway

It's a difficult process, but I really don't see any other way for you to attain the healing you need. Grit your teeth and do it. I can't make this any plainer. Just as you cannot take a drink only once a month to wean yourself off alcohol, so you cannot stop an addictive relationship without a clean break.

See a professional counselor

We're not wonder workers, but we can help you through critical decisions. Through our training and experience, we have some insights to share about the nature of relationships, what's healthy, what's not, and what might be stopping you from making a clean break.

Find a counselor you're comfortable with. Ask friends for their recommendations, but you should also ask your pastor or doctor for referrals. If you feel uncomfortable with a counselor you visit, say so. The counselor may learn to accommodate your needs in a better way or may refer you to someone who matches your needs better. Remember, it is always up to you to choose a counselor, go to your sessions, communicate what you need, and ultimately change. You can see how well a particular counselor helps you gain some insights and then try a different counselor if you like. It's up to you, but you should seek help.

Put up strong boundaries and live by them

Let me say again: the best recovery is still cold turkey. But if you absolutely cannot make a clean break, at least try to put the brakes on the addiction by setting limits.

Consider limiting your physical relationship, your amount of time together, the money that you spend on the other person (or is spent on you), or the areas in which you rely on the other person. If you have determined that you or your partner is over-dependent in some area, make up your mind to change that area. It is a matter of treating the symptoms, but it may help.

Avoid drugs and alcohol

This is a dangerous time for you. If you are addicted to a relationship, you are very suspectible to other addictions. I have known many who have let their dissatisfaction with their relationships, and their inability to break free, drive them to drink or drugs. These substances, of course, just make things worse. These cross-addictions are very common among individuals with addictive personalities.

If you are experiencing physical or sexual abuse, get out and get help

In some severe cases of relationship addiction, husbands regularly beat their wives, and the wives feel powerless to change things. If this is your situation, you are not doing anyone a favor by keeping silent. Your husband needs help and so do you. If children are involved, they *definitely* need help.

Many communities have special hotlines for battered women. (Often they are listed in the "blue pages" of the phone book.) Call one of them, or call the police (especially in violent or dangerous situations). Consult with your pastor and/or other church leaders. Ask your doctor to recommend an agency that might help. Do not keep the secret any longer.

6. WHEN YOU'RE OUT OF AN ADDICTIVE RELATIONSHIP (POINT 6 ON FIG. 1)

Let't say you've done it. You've recognized your addiction and taken the necessary steps to get out of the problem relationship. Great! But you're not out of the woods yet. Relapse is common unless you remain vigilant. Continue to gather the strength you need to stay free—from your ex-partner and from new addictive relationships.

In our story, Frank was tempted several times to go back to help the others, even after he was free and sprinting for safety. He heard Evie's cries and even turned around once. But then he remembered it was impossible for Evie and him to work together. He had to get out on his own.

Stay away from your ex-partner

As I said before, it's tempting to be "just friends." But it doesn't work. You see, in most cases it's not just an addiction to a *romance* with that person; it's an addiction to a *friendship*, too. You have learned to rely on that person for all sorts of things, and after the breakup, you will miss that person terribly. You might assume that if the romance is ended, the danger of addiction is gone, and so the friendship can continue. But, no, the addiction can go on in the friendship, and that may lead you back into a romance.

One young couple I counseled had just broken off an unhealthy romance but continued (against my advice) to see each other as friends. Jenny had initiated the breakup, which had hurt Will deeply, but she felt sorry for him and still invited him for dinner each week. On one occasion, Jenny (perhaps missing their old times together) rekindled the sexual flame, and they ended up in bed. Will left even more confused and distraught than before. They have since agreed that it's best to stay away from each other entirely. It is just too difficult for them to maintain proper boundaries.

Don't rationalize—just stay away!

I've known people who planned to "accidentally" bump into the former lover. They missed the relationship and wanted to see the person, but they wanted to assure themselves they were still going cold turkey. So they'd drive by the person's house or office and ultimately arrange to meet.

Will was one of those people. He had left a bunch of stuff at

Jenny's place, and so each week or so, he had an excuse to go back and fetch something—and to see her, of course. "Just make one trip," I told him. "Take a big box and get all your stuff out of there." But he felt he needed that excuse.

He kept in touch with Jenny's friends. If they were going out somewhere together, he would just "happen" to show up there. The truth was, he was continuing to feed his addiction. Part of him agreed that cold turkey was the way to go, but another part kept lying to himself, finding flimsy excuses to see Jenny again.

"What does it hurt?" Will asked me. "I just saw Jenny briefly. Nothing happened. I needed to see her. What's the problem with that?"

"You're addicted," I replied. "Try saying the same thing, but substitute the word *cocaine* for *Jenny*."

He tried it. "What does it hurt?" he said tentatively. "I just . . . did a little cocaine. I needed it. What's the problem with that?"

We looked at each other, and he recognized the problem. It is foolish and dangerous to continue seeing the object of your addiction. Stay away, and don't kid yourself.

Admit your ongoing addictive tendency

A helpful insight from Twelve-Step groups is that you continue to be an addict even when you've kicked the habit. You are in recovery, but you're still susceptible.

Even when you leave an addictive relationship, you carry a susceptibility to relational addictions. You must be careful about future relationships—perhaps even twenty years from now.

Reject the rebound

When a well-meaning friend says, "You need a new love in your life," say, "No, I don't!" Rebound relationships can sneak up on you. You will face great emotional and social pressure to get involved again. Don't do it.

"This new guy will make you forget all about Richard."

"One date with Sheila and your feelings for Marie are history."

Don't buy it. It's like taking heroin to forget about cocaine, like swilling gin to kick your vodka habit. It doesn't help.

Take time to heal

People want instant cures for long-term problems. I've known people who took twenty years to develop a smoking habit, and they want to be cured in twenty minutes. Sure, God works miracles. But the miracle of healing usually takes place over a period of time. Relationship addiction is no different.

I work with people recovering from divorce. They are often amazed when I recommend that they wait at least two years before starting a new romance. Two years! You'd think I just asked them to enter a monastery. But the truth is that most people aren't ready to reenter the dating world for about two years, and for some, it should be longer. If your addictive relationship was long-term, a marriage or something like it, that might be a good benchmark for you. Use those two years to recover, to build your self-image, to build healthy friendships, but not to find a new lover.

If your relationship was of shorter duration or less serious, a shorter recovery period is necessary—perhaps six months to a year. Think of it this way: as long as it took you to get into that relationship, it will probably take you that long to get out.

Watch out for other forms of addiction

Now that you're living without your addictive relationship, drugs, alcohol, gambling, pornography, food, and other addictive substances may try to ensnare you.

Develop a positive program for yourself

So far, I've been saying, "Don't . . . don't . . . watch out . . ." Here's one more caution: don't dwell on the negative. Devise a plan to put yourself back together. Go to the gym on a regular basis. Read the books you've always wanted to read. Start a Thursday night video party to catch up on the classics. Get out your old guitar and try to remember the chords.

This is a time to rebuild yourself. Whatever your action plan, tackle it with all your might.

Rebuild friendships and social supports

You need close friends more than ever. If you have alienated old friends, try to restore those friendships. Send a card or give a call. Say, "I'm sorry. I'm back."

Get involved with groups, too. Enlarge your circle of acquaintances. Singles groups become a great deal of fun when you stop trying to hook someone of the opposite sex. But don't limit yourself to singles groups. There are service organizations, softball teams, study groups, bowling leagues, community theaters, political campaigns, and neighborhood groups to join.

Develop safe friendships with the opposite sex

You may not be ready immediately. You may go through a "men are jerks" or "women are stupid" phase. But maybe six months after your breakup, you should make it a point to get to know someone of the opposite sex in a safe, nonromantic way so that you can restore a positive image of the other gender. Some men can really listen to you. Some women can be brilliant. There are men who can talk about things other than sports. There are women who can be honest with you. That may be hard to believe in the wake of your breakup, but you need to learn that eventually.

Get in touch with your purpose in life

Think about why you're here. On the earth. Living life. If you're a Christian, your answer will probably have something to do with God—glorifying Him, enjoying Him. And even if you're not, it may have to do with others—reaching out and helping other people.

You don't need to come up with a well-defined purpose statement unless you enjoy doing that sort of thing. I expect that there will always be some mysteries concerning our existence here, even though we may have a general idea of what we're about. But think about your purpose.

Then when you've thought about it, *do something* in keeping with it. Do a good deed for a neighbor. Go grocery shopping for the older woman next door. Buy a Big Mac for the homeless person on the street. Encourage a troubled family member. Teach an inner-city kid to count to ten.

Go to church and sing God's praises for all you're worth. Spend extra time in prayer for the needs of those around you. Find a winsome way to let your coworkers know of God's love.

Acts like these can get you in the right groove again. They can remind you of how valuable you are. They can anchor you and keep you from sliding down Addiction Canyon again.

Chapter Eleven

CASE STUDY: LAURIE

Laurie is an exception. Most addictions have deep-seated causes, but Laurie's came on suddenly. Most carry ongoing dangers, but Laurie's struggle now seems to be finished. We might call it a catastrophic addiction. Her life was not an addiction waiting to happen. But it happened anyway. Her case reminds us that anyone can succumb to a relationship addiction and anyone can heal from it.

She sits in my office now, not as a counselee, but as a former client and a former member of our relationship group (from chapter 1). She's telling me her story again, for this book, hoping it helps others. It has been two years since the group ended. She is the picture of a confident, healthy, whole person. The events she describes are struggles she's faced over the past five years. Only within the last year or so, she says, has she finally put them behind her.

BREAKING THE RULES

In her mid-forties, Laurie has been married and divorced twice. Her first husband was a philanderer. She remains friends

142

with her second—that marriage "just didn't work out." Her addiction began shortly after her second divorce.

She is quick to say that she was not "on the rebound." Her second marriage had been crumbling for a while. She is well aware of the slippery slope of divorce recovery, and she says she was through that. She was not a wreck at the time. No, she seemed healthy and well adjusted as she reentered single life. "I was not emotionally vulnerable," she says now, looking back. "I thought I knew what I was doing. Well, I was wrong."

Forced to support herself, Laurie got a job in a financial consulting office where she learned the ropes quickly. There she met Alan.

Alan was a hunk. He had a winning personality and a sense of humor that made him a good businessman—and popular with the ladies. He was no flashy flirt, either. He seemed sincerely interested in people, especially in Laurie. When he asked her out, she couldn't believe her good fortune.

"I broke my own rule," she says. "'Never get involved with anyone you work with.' I should have known better."

But he was overwhelming, saying the right things, doing the right things. Their romance blossomed. They dated about six months, and then they moved in together.

"It was good for a few months after that," Laurie says. "But then he started to withdraw. He would do things on his own without telling me. He wouldn't include me in things." Alan had an opportunity to buy a house at a good price. That was his excuse to move out, though they continued their relationship.

"He was great at mixed messages. When he was with me, he said all the things I wanted to hear. He was a master at that. But there were many things he wasn't telling me."

Like he was seeing someone else.

Laurie discovered that a month after he moved out. She was furious: "He didn't deny it. He didn't defend himself. He didn't do anything. That's the way he is." Laurie's voice is calm as she describes those events, but her tone bears the scars of a lot of hurt.

She had run headlong into that maddening male passivity.

From his perspective, he had made no promises. She had assumed his unmixed devotion. He was free to date others, as was she.

But she wasn't. Her heart was wrapped around his life. She was addicted. It was at that point in the relationship that Laurie joined our group in order to gain the strength to detach emotionally from Alan.

He continued to "waltz in and out" of Laurie's life for the next six months. She saw him daily at work, and they dated occasionally. Their times together were great; he was charming as usual. But there was always the specter of those "other women" he was seeing. She wanted him all to herself. Whenever they did go out, she'd feel great for a few days and then fall apart. She had the sense that she was a second choice for him, and yet she longed to be with him. Her self-esteem, normally quite healthy, was sliding.

Then he stopped asking Laurie out. There was one "other woman" he wanted to focus his attention on. He would not be dating Laurie anymore.

She was destroyed. Though, in retrospect, it may have been the best thing for her, at the time she was devastated: "I could not sleep. I developed a cough that I couldn't get rid of. My hair started falling out. I had a horrible feeling in my chest and in my stomach. I was frequently under medication and very suicidal. I used to pray, 'Lord, if You love me, put me out of my misery.' I wanted to die more than anything because I just didn't want to face the pain. I remember screaming at the Lord, punching the walls, hitting my head against the walls, scratching my face, doing things that seem totally bizarre to me now."

At that point, Laurie was still in our group, but she started individual counseling as well.

THE ROAD TO RECOVERY

What do you say to such a person? You basically try to empower her to pick herself up and start over, to make the hard decisions she needs to make. You try to help her get a realistic perspective on her life and relationships. You assure her of her personal worth. You put her in contact with other people facing similar struggles.

Laurie's pain was intensified by the fact that she worked closely with Alan. He also lived down the street from her. And he wanted to remain friends with her. It was all smiles in the office, though inside Laurie was burning up.

My normal cold turkey advice would be to get a new job and move away. But Laurie wouldn't do either one. She had a good job. She had risen in the company and now commanded an impressive salary. Throughout the crisis, her performance at work had not suffered. She prided herself on that. She felt like a "slimeball" in the rest of her life, but she still acted with confidence at work. It was a bit of certainty she did not want to give up.

So the next solution was to close the door to any future romantic involvement with Alan. He had waltzed through her heart with abandon for the last year. Even though he had rejected her, he was not burning any bridges. She felt the distinct possibility that he might come back to her if his current relationship foundered. She secretly hoped that he would.

But that would just put her back on the roller coaster, back into the addiction. *She* needed to break from him, to slam the door. Otherwise she would never be free.

One winter day, Laurie went through her home and picked up every item that belonged to Alan. She put everything in a big box. It was a purging of the last year of her life. Every remnant of his life with her was piled in that box. He did not belong in her home anymore. She drove down the street to his house and deposited the box at his door.

That was a major act in her recovery. But one thing remained. Alan had a key to her place. She needed to get it back. It seemed like such a trifle. He certainly wouldn't use it since he had moved on to another relationship. There was no danger involved. But that key was a symbol of something much greater—his right to reenter her life romantically. I urged her to get the key back. She assured me she would.

But she forgot. And she forgot again. And she forgot again. She saw him frequently at work, but she didn't ask for the key. "I think part of me wanted him to have that key," Laurie says now.

About a month after she left the box at his door, Laurie asked Alan for her key. It was a few more weeks before she got it. A chapter of her life had finally ended.

And a new one began. Recovery. The healing of her heart. It's not easy when the scab is regularly ripped open at work. She observes, "Being in an addictive relationship is the worst thing I can think of. It's worse than being on drugs, I think. It's awful to have to see a person every day, someone you really care about and really love, and to know that that person is going on with his life without you. I don't know how I got through it. I had a lot of people there who loved me and supported me, and God was there."

Laurie began to keep a journal, which was a helpful outlet for her feelings. She also found our group sessions beneficial. She drew strength from the encouragement of others who were in the same boat. But it has been, literally, a day-to-day struggle. Alan continued his winsome ways at work. And Laurie never knew when she would see him with another woman as she drove by his house.

It has been about two years since Laurie finally got her key back. Her healing has been slow but sure.

Alan was away from the office a few months, and that was good. But he came back.

Then he was having problems with his steady girlfriend, and that was bad. Laurie says, "He had the nerve to ask me out again. It was all I could do to say no." It was what she had dreamed of earlier, her second chance with the man she loved. But she had made some hard choices by that time. The door was closed. She admits, "It hadn't stopped hurting; I just made up my mind that this relationship could not be. Maybe at that point it was my pride. I just couldn't let him yank me around like that anymore."

Now she seems strong again, brimming with self-esteem. She

still sees Alan at the office. "I am able to work with him and it doesn't hurt," she tells me as she sits in my office. "I even get annoyed with him sometimes." She says she recently worked closely on a project with him and felt no emotional pain. It's over.

HINDSIGHT

"If I had gone cold turkey, not seeing him at all," she says, "it would have been painful, but the healing would not have lasted this long. With cold turkey, you have the blessing of not having to see the person or talk to him or know what's going on in his life. I didn't have that option. I was exposed to it every day."

She seems to have gained confidence through the ordeal. And she is in no hurry for a new romance. "I have no intention of ever having any repeats," she laughs.

"I have some pretty close relationships with some men," she goes on, "but they're not romantic. I haven't met anybody I desire to have a romantic relationship with. I think my expectations are much higher. I'm at the point where I see dysfunctional behavior or some quirk in a man, and I just don't pursue it."

Laurie speaks about the boundaries she has discovered. She will not lose herself in a man again: "I'm okay on my own. I wouldn't mind being in a relationship, but I don't need it. I'm who I am, and I'm happy with who I am now. I just got to the point where I said, 'Okay, you have to be a healthy person and be happy with Laurie whether there's someone else in your life or not.' "

She says she can sympathize with people who are in similar situations. She'd like to use her experience to help people who are hurting, "whether through divorce or the loss of a child, because I think I have a lot to give. I've walked on the hot coals for a long time, and I've learned an awful lot. I want to give it back."

What advice does she give to someone who is where she was, wrestling with a relationship addiction?

She states, "I would tell you to quit, to get as far away from the situation as you possibly can. If that's not an option, I'd urge you to talk to a professional counselor. You need a group of friends who can encourage you, friends who are honest enough to tell you the truth whether you want to hear it or not. Also, pray a lot. Put your life in God's hands because sometimes it takes God a long time to answer—but He does answer. And be strong—realize that you have a lot of value as a human being and you have a lot of value in the eyes of God. Look for ways that this can make you stronger.

"As difficult as this was for me, I think God used it to bring me closer to Him."

EVALUATION

Laurie has no serious addiction in her family history. But she does seem to have some compulsion to be in a romantic relationship. Her recent troubles have scared her away from such relationships for a while, but this is the longest she has ever gone "without a man."

Her difficulty with Alan could be due to her idealization of him. She looked up to him professionally and admired him physically. Her need for a relationship allowed her to ignore the mistreatment she received from Alan—things she *never* would have tolerated from either husband. This confirms a point we've been seeing: addictive relationships are irrational. They can't always be explained, and they rarely make sense. By all appearances, Laurie should have been able to stand up to Alan and avoid the complications. Why didn't she? That's one of the irrationalities.

But there is hope. Laurie has come through this struggle to become a stronger person. That can happen to many others in similar situations. With professional help, the support of close friends, and an awareness of personal value and purpose in life, wounded ones can truly break the addictive grip and come back to health and freedom.

_____ *Chapter Twelve* _____

BEST FRIENDS

The coach yells from the first-base line: "See yourself hitting the ball, Joey! See that level swing! See yourself making contact!"

I was searching for a way to start this chapter, to zero in on the importance of at least maintaining an image of healthy love. And there it was, happening at a softball game. The coach had obviously coached Joey before—he was reminding him to keep his right elbow up, to keep his eye on the ball. But then he said, "See yourself hitting the ball," and I had my hook.

There's that whole sports theory of psychocybernetics. The idea is that your body conforms to what you see or what you imagine yourself seeing. Even if you don't know how to move all those muscles in just the right way, your body knows, and it will perform properly if you only give it a proper image.

I don't know if that's a valid sports strategy or not. (In Joey's case, he must have seen himself hitting a pop-up to the short-stop.) But it *is* a valid relationship strategy.

Many people have faulty relationships because they don't know any better. They have never seen a healthy relationship in action. You have seen this in the case studies—people are repeat-

149

ing the dysfunctions of their birth families. Girls crave attention from their fathers and grow up to crave attention from their husbands. Men are self-centered rogues and women are stupid servants—that's all some people have ever known.

As you strive to develop and maintain healthy relationships, you need to have good images in front of you. Find couples with solid marriages, and see how they do it. Stop watching the TV shows about dysfunctional families, and try to find shows that portray mutually committed relationships (good luck!). Read the rest of this chapter to see what relational health really looks like. And then *see yourself* in a healthy relationship.

I've heard too many preachers expound on, say, the book of Isaiah with eighteen points, all beginning with the letter *T*. What began as a helpful memory hook turned into a bizarre word game. I'm not trying to do this here, but I do want you to remember these points so that you can use them from time to time to see yourself in a good relationship. So here goes.

Good relationships are characterized by best friendship (chapter 12), balance (chapter 13), and boundaries (chapter 14). We'll talk first about being your partner's best friend.

Healthy romances are also good friendships. Sad to say, this isn't true of all romances. You probably know people who say about their partners:

- "He is really exciting to be with, but I don't feel that I know him at all."
- "She's a lot of fun to date, but I don't really trust her."
- "I love the way she looks, but I don't understand her. When we talk, it's like we're in different worlds."
- "I feel so afraid when I'm with him. I can't really be myself."

Romantic attraction is a capricious thing; it flies on whims and impulse. The ancients depicted the god Cupid firing his arrows, often at random. If you fall in love with someone who's good for you, you're lucky. When relationships are built on these feelings, they are not sturdy. They can crash with the first strong wind.

But how do friendships happen? Usually, you find someone among your acquaintances who shares your interests. Perhaps you find that you think alike in certain areas or that your personalities are complementary. Consciously or subconsciously, you decide to spend more time together, to share more deeply of yourself, to listen to and care for the other. The friendship grows on such sharing. Friendships, grown and nurtured through time, can weather all sorts of difficulties.

You *can* have both—romance and friendship. Many couples have started out in torrid romances, only to have those feelings fade. But in the place of romantic feelings, they discover that a new friendship has been forged. It doesn't happen automatically. It requires communication, trust, and committed love.

COMMUNICATION

Best friends can talk about anything and everything. Each shows interest in the other's life and feels free to express personal feelings. Each one understands how the other person's mind works. They don't always agree, but they understand their disagreements. They don't get hung up on petty quarrels because each knows where the other is coming from.

Volumes have been written on the art of communication. If you're having problems communicating with your partner, consult one of them. We don't have room here for a full treatment, but let me suggest some areas that might require attention.

First, at least half of the communication process is *listening*. That goes without saying, right? But I'm amazed at how many couples get in trouble because they stop listening to each other. Sometimes we assume we know what the other person is saying, so we tune out. Sometimes we are so concerned about making our point that we never focus on the other's words. Sometimes we read negative motives into the other person's statements, and we react defensively to imaginary attacks.

"Stop, look, and listen" might be a catchphrase for healthy relationships. Good listeners are not afraid to say, "Would you repeat that?" or "What do you mean by that?" in an effort to clarify the statement they've heard. They may repeat the statement in a different way to make sure they've got it right: "Do you really mean to say that you think baseball is the most beautiful game ever invented?"

Second, good communicators know how to make *I-statements*. An I-statement says how I feel without attributing motives or feelings to anyone else. If I say, "You're so selfish!" I'm setting us up for a fight. But if I turn that into an I-statement—"When I see you act that way, I feel that you don't care about me"—we can deal peacefully with the problem. My partner is not on the defensive. On the contrary, I have made myself vulnerable.

My partner could respond, "Well, you're imagining things as usual," or "You're just too sensitive." But I'm banking on the fact that my partner is as interested as I am in resolving our conflicts. I'm giving her the benefit of the doubt. I'm implying, "I believe you *do* care about me, even though I'm not reading that in your behavior. So either I'm reading you wrong, or you're not expressing your love for me. Let's work on this together." (If your partner consistently responds to your I-statements with further attacks on you, perhaps these assumptions are *not* true. In that case, your problem is greater than poor communication.)

The I-statement brings the discussion back to the basics of where I am, what I feel. It also allows for the possibility that I may be wrong in my interpretation of the other person's actions or words. It's an important tactic in any couple's attempt to maintain good communication.

Some people say, "We don't need to talk. We know each other so well, we read each other's mind." Maybe so, but I doubt it. That sounds to me like unrealistic romanticizing. It's good to talk anyway. It can be terribly frustrating when you *think* you're reading your partner's mind, but your translation is dead wrong. And it can be threatening to have your mind read. (I saw a cartoon once in which a character said, "I know you think you know what I thought when I said that, but I really thought something else, I think.") For a healthy relationship, you need to keep talking—if only to verify and calibrate your mind-reading skills.

In his witty drama *Our Town*, Thornton Wilder presents a middle-aged couple having breakfast on their son's wedding day. Dr. Gibbs says, "Julia, do you know one of the things I was scared of when I married you? . . . I was afraid we wouldn't have material for conversation more'n'd last us a few weeks."

They laugh together, and he adds, "Well, you and I been conversing for twenty years now without any noticeable barren spells."

"Well," his wife answers, "good weather, bad weather—'tain't very choice, but I always find something to say."

Granted, some people are gifted conversationalists; others aren't. But communication is essential to the health of a relationship. It doesn't have to be smooth or witty or entertaining or deeply sensitive. But it does need to happen. It's worth working at.

TRUST AND HONOR

Friendship involves *trust*. A friend can share something deeply personal, perhaps something shocking, with a friend—and can trust that the other person will remain loyal. Healthy relationships are based on that kind of trust and loyalty.

I'm not saying that you put your mind on hold. I'm not saying that you ignore dangerous situations. If your friend says he's beginning to use drugs, you will express your friendship by trying to help him stop. You don't need to approve of bad behavior. But there's a commitment to the person.

You may have heard the saying, oft-quoted by Christians: "Hate the sin, love the sinner." That's what I'm talking about here. You may need to express concern over some actions or attitudes, but a true friend also expresses acceptance of the person.

When trust exists between two partners in a romantic relationship, openness and honesty are present. If I can trust you with my secrets, I will begin to open up my innermost self to you. I will not be afraid that I'm not good enough for you. I will share myself with you.

In one of our case studies, Sally spoke of "not being herself" with one man she dated. He was out of her league, she felt, and she was always trying to live up to his standards. There was no openness. She did not trust him with her true self, and thus she maintained an off-balance relationship.

Obviously, trust is a two-way street. You need to earn my trust, and I yours. (In Sally's case, her lawyer friend had obviously not earned her trust; she would have been foolish to trust him with any more of herself. But that is a symptom of an unhealthy relationship.) We earn trust by being loyal, by accepting, by (here's a key word) *honoring* the other person.

Do you know couples who honor each other? Isn't that wonderful to see? You'll be talking to one partner, and he'll say, "You really ought to ask my wife about that; she's brilliant on that subject." Or she'll say, "My husband did the sweetest thing. Let me tell you . . ." Yes, even that can go to extremes when people dote on each other. But how refreshing it is to see that upbuilding going on! And just imagine what happens at home. One says, "Honey, I think you ought to go ahead and take that art class. I think you'd be good at that." The other says, "I'm sorry you didn't get that promotion. You earned it."

You may also have met couples who take every opportunity to tear each other down. She'll give you play-by-play of his latest business failure. He'll make snide comments about her clothes, her looks, and her age. They make everybody feel uncomfortable. You don't want to imagine their home life.

Most of us have fragile self-esteem. We bruise easily. Every time we open our mouths, we make ourselves vulnerable. Every time we say something about what's inside us, we hand someone a knife. No wonder there are so many fearful people. They may be in relationships, but they feel lonely because they have never felt secure enough to share what's inside.

It's easy to tear others down, but it's rewarding to build them up. In healthy relationships, partners honor each other, and by doing so, they coax each other out of a shell. They inspire trust and openness and honesty.

These attributes don't come all at once. Trust builds slowly, very slowly if one's self-esteem is fragile or recently crushed. But at least a germ of it exists in every healthy relationship.

SELF-GIVING LOVE

My colleague Tom Jones, in his fine book *The Single-Again Handbook*, tells of a man who was leaving his wife, Margie, for a new love, Beth. The man spoke of how he hadn't "felt anything" for Margie for two years and how Beth was giving him great new feelings.

Jones challenged him: Would these great new feelings last?

The man didn't know. He figured, "You just have to go with the feelings you have at the present."

"What is this feeling you have for Beth?" Jones asked. "Is it love?"

"If this isn't love," the man responded, "then I don't know what love is."

Jones concluded that the man was right—he didn't know what love was. Within two years he had divorced Beth and was asking Margie to take him back.

The story could be repeated in millions of homes. It's symptomatic of a deep problem: we don't know what love is.

A lot of what we call love is just shared enjoyment: "I love you because you make me feel so good, but when that feeling stops, babe—when you get wrinkles or I get bored—I'm out of here."

A lot of "love" is actually bargaining. I may be doing something nice for my partner, but I have an ulterior motive. I'm looking for a payback. I'll do the dishes for her so that she won't put up a fuss when I have to go to that meeting tonight. In a long-term relationship, I learn what I have to do to get along. There's nothing wrong with getting along; it's just not the essence of love.

Various writers have looked for the meaning of love in ancient Greek words. They had four different words for different aspects of what we call love. The first, *storge*, is simple enjoyment. I can "love" broccoli, cats, or baseball. The second, *eros*, is sexual "love," the physical desire we might feel for someone attractive to us. The third is *philia*, friendship. We tend to like those who are like us. In a way, in casual friendships we are loving ourselves, bonding with those who are going in the same direction as we are. You may have had friendships in your life that you thought were pretty sturdy, but they crumbled when someone moved away or changed or got irked over some trivial matter. *Philia* is good, it's a kind of "love," but it's not the ultimate.

The final Greek word for love is one embraced by the Christians, *agape*. This is the way God loves humans and the way He wants us to love each other. It is love with no selfishness, no bargaining, no expectation of reward. It is a totally *giving* love.

Jesus spent His earthly ministry defining and embodying this love. One night He gave His disciples His ultimate command: "Love one another as I have loved you." How's that? He went on to say, "Greater love has no one than this, than to lay down one's life for his friends" (John 15:12–13).

He used the word *agape* there for "love" and a form of *philia* for "friends." He was taking the concept of friendship and kicking it to a higher level: "You may be all cozy in this casual friendship thing with Me, Peter, James, John, and you others, but I'm going to give My life for you. That's how much I care for you. *And I want you to love each other in that same way, giving yourselves to them.*"

That's the best friendship of healthy relationships—not a casual shared-interest acquaintance, but a self-giving love.

Some people call this unconditional love. That's a great concept, but I think it invites misunderstanding. It is true that partners should love each other in a totally giving way, not to receive anything in return. The misunderstanding arises when we confuse unconditional love with codependency. True love looks out for the best interests of the other person. Thus, it can be tough love. It can call the other person to accountability. Love does not enable people to carry on self-destructive behaviors. It empowers them to change; it inspires them to step forward; but it is patient as they stumble along.

This is evident even in God's love for us. Yes, He loves us unconditionally despite the things we do that displease Him. But He also draws us into a life of obedience. He holds us accountable for our behavior. He asks us to respond in faith and repentance. While His loving acts on our behalf are freely given with no strings attached, we miss out on the joy of a loving relationship with Him if we do not respond in love.

It's the same way with human relationships. One person can love another unconditionally, sacrificing and slaving for that person. But for that *relationship* to work, to fly, to be full of joy, the love has to go both ways. We'll discuss that later in more detail.

Healthy relationships, whether romantic or not, have this self-giving love coming from both partners. A relationship changes from a 50–50 arrangement to 100–100. Not 100–0, in which one person does all the work, but 100–100. *Both* are willing, but neither has to.

You may have seen 50–50 relationships in action: "I will do this for you, but you'd better do that for me because I've done other things for you and it's just not fair." People like that are always keeping score. And usually, the score is tilted in their favor. He may forget some of the great things she's done for him, but he places great importance on some trivial things he's done.

"Whaddayamean I don't do anything? I washed the dishes tonight, didn't I?"

"Well, you should. They're your dishes. You decided you wanted an ice-cream sundae in the middle of the night."

"It was just because you didn't serve dessert with dinner."

"It was a rich meal anyway. I slaved over that thing. Not that you'd notice."

"Don't give me that. I work hard all day to put that food on the table."

"And I don't work hard?"

Both partners are convinced that *they* give 60 percent or more to the relationship, and they're not getting enough in return. But when they commit themselves to self-giving love, they are not concerned about giving more than the other person because they're not keeping score. Their focus is on their commitment and what they can give, which frees them up to appreciate what they are getting.

So that's the first thing to remember about healthy relationships. They are best friendships in which both partners communicate, trust, and honor each other, and are committed to self-giving love with no requirement for a payback.

_____ *Chapter Thirteen* _____

BALANCE

Imagine this. You work as a boatperson at Harry's Honeymoon Haven, a resort at one of the lakes near Niagara Falls. All sorts of couples come to the resort, which features an idyllic rowboat ride across the beautiful lake. It is your job to row the boat. The husband sits at one end, the wife at the other, and you're in the middle rowing. That's not the most romantic arrangement, but, hey, go with me on this—I'm making it up as I go along.

In your vast experience ferrying couples across the lake, you've had to deal with various issues of balance. Sometimes husbands are huge and wives are small, or vice versa. You compensate by moving slightly toward the lighter person, evening the load somewhat. There have been some challenges, especially when the circus was in town, but you have always been able to maintain balance on your boat.

But then you meet Big George Bumpus and his wife, Tiny. You can sense there will be trouble. It's not that the weight differential is so great, but Big George has been drinking. His breath smells of whiskey, and he keeps calling you Ferdinand for

159

some odd reason, which apparently goes back to his bullfighting days.

Big George staggers to your boat, flashing a wad of bills and insisting that you show him this lovely lake. You protest, but he's already in the boat, and you figure it would be more trouble to get him out. So you help Tiny into the small craft and position yourself on her side of the center, and you row out toward the middle of the lake. So far, so good.

But then Big George starts to imagine things. Mosquitoes the size of Brahma bulls or something like that. In his unstable condition, he lurches to the side—and that does it. The boat capsizes. Only the life preserver and your lifeguard training save Big George's life. Tiny swims safely to shore and is never seen again.

Relationships are like that. They find a certain equilibrium. We have all seen couples in which one partner seems stronger than the other. That's not necessarily bad. Often one person will have a stronger personality; the other might be more submissive by nature. My friend Bill is like that. He is easygoing and soft-spoken, while his wife, Melanie, is a dynamo. She is vivacious and talented, full of ideas and energy. At first glance, you might think this relationship is seriously out of balance. How can he allow himself to be dominated like that? But as I've gotten to know Bill and Melanie, I've gained a great appreciation for the quality of their marriage. Bill doesn't say much, but when he speaks, Melanie pays attention. And he is comfortable with Melanie's exuberance. They complement each other. As long as each is giving love and nurturing the other, it's beautiful. Even with disparate personalities, adjustments can be made to create a workable balance in a relationship—as we saw with the rowboat.

But a partner who is out of balance *personally* threatens the balance of the relationship. That becomes an unhealthy situation and a dangerous one. In the boat story, Big George had a problem. It wasn't Tiny's problem—except that she had married him. It wasn't your problem—except that you were in the middle of a lake with him. His problem created a problem for the whole boat—just as one partner's personal problem creates a problem for the whole relationship.

Healthy relationships are well balanced, and the people within them are well balanced.

PERSONAL BALANCE

All of us are collections of disparate elements. We are strong and weak. We are confident and insecure. We are extroverted and introverted.

I recently took a personality profile test. They ask you a bunch of questions, you tell them what you're like, and they turn around and tell you what you just told them. Brilliant!

But seriously, I like that this particular test rated me on a scale. It didn't say, "You are a feeler rather than a thinker." It said, "You're about a 62 percent on the feeler side of the thinker-feeler scale." That's an important difference because I *am* a thinker. I just tend to give my feelings priority—roughly 62 percent of the time.

As I said, all of us are combinations of qualities. Personal balance comes from accepting *all* of who we are, the minority as well as the majority. I need to express my thinking side as well as my feeling side. It's a matter of *wholeness*. If I deny a part of who I am, I am unwhole.

"Whole" people keep work and play in proper perspective. They don't live for the weekend, but neither do they live at their jobs.

Whole people enjoy family life, but they also have friends outside the family, and they can be comfortable by themselves.

Whole people can set some ambitious goals for themselves, but they are aware of their limitations. They push themselves at a reasonable rate.

Whole people give freely of themselves—their time, their concern, their resources—to others, but they also guard their wholeness. They are aware when they are burning out. They can say no before they have no more to give.

Whole people can function independently of others, but they choose to make themselves somewhat dependent on those they love. They create an *inter*dependence with others on which good relationships are built.

Whole people are aware of their spirituality. They have a healthy relationship with God, but they also live out their faith in practical ways. They accept and enjoy the physicality of human life.

Whole people do not let addictions throw them out of balance. They avoid substance abuse since it would limit their capacities, making them less whole. They guard against other behavioral addictions, such as gambling or pornography, because these activities put artificial emphasis on one small aspect of a person and deny the rest.

Whole people can enjoy themselves in a variety of pleasurable pursuits, but they don't put undue importance on a momentary high. They keep looking at the big picture of a satisfying lifestyle.

All of that may seem ideal to you. It may seem out of reach, unrealistic. But it's not. There are many well-balanced people around. I'm not talking about perfection; we all have our faults. But many people find an individual equilibrium and live in healthy ways. Others are moving toward that equilibrium.

BALANCE OF ASPECTS

Relationships have various aspects—mental, spiritual, physical, social, personal. Sometimes couples major on one aspect and ignore the others.

This emphasis happens most commonly with the physical aspect. Our society prizes physical attraction; that is where most of our bonding starts. But how many couples have based their whole relationship on "you look great and you're a fantastic sexual partner"? They wake up one day and realize that they don't really know each other at all. Their personalities conflict, they don't think the same way, and they embarrass each other in public. It's out of balance.

I tell couples who are still dating that if you jump into physical involvement with each other, you are already building an unbalanced relationship. You can't possibly know each other that intimately on a mental or spiritual level, but you are zooming ahead with the physical. Slow down and grow together in all areas as you head toward committed love. Keep things in balance.

Some might emphasize the social aspect of their relationship. They complement each other in public. People comment that they belong together, they're a great team. But get them alone and they can't stand each other. Or perhaps they have major spiritual or intellectual differences.

There will always be people who are naturally more intellectual or more spiritually astute or more socially active. But in the best relationships, couples seek to strengthen the areas where they're naturally weak. They work at knowing each other in those other uncharted territories.

BALANCE BETWEEN PARTNERS

Katie fell in love with Bob in college. He was witty and bright, and they thought alike on many things. They could talk together for hours. She felt she understood him better than others did, and she found his ideas stimulating.

After they dated for a while, Bob told Katie about a medical problem that sometimes affected his behavior. He was on medication, but she needed to understand his plight and allow for it. She assured him that she would. Eventually, they moved in together.

But Bob became quite demanding. He had a hard time finding and keeping a job. She would encourage him, type resumes, scour the want ads, and send him out the door. When he did land a job, he would sour on it in a few months.

In their relationship, whenever Bob did something wrong, he blamed it on his medical problem. Whenever he wanted something from her, he appealed to her sense of pity. Through it all, Katie felt unappreciated. Nobody was taking care of *her*.

She realized that the relationship was out of balance. It was all about Bob and his problem. She was just there to help him cope. Feeling overwhelmed by him and his needs, she asked him to move out, though they would continue to date.

As a painter, she had an opportunity to show some paintings at a gallery in a distant city. She traveled there for the opening, a major event in her life and career. To her dismay, Bob did not call to wish her luck before she left. When he did call, four days after she returned, he talked about what he had been doing—nothing about her trip.

That was the end of the relationship. She broke up with him shortly afterward, and he could not understand why.

Katie was more than willing to give Bob the care and support he needed. But she needed something in return. The relationship was dangerously out of balance, and that was throwing her out of balance personally. She was wise to get out of it.

A healthy relationship is not about him, and it's not about her—it's about them. The partners recognize certain times when one may need to support the other, but there's a healthy give-and-take, and the balance is restored soon afterward. In public, they talk about each other, and they use "us" and "we" a lot. (Out-of-balance relationships usually have one partner saying "me" a lot and the other saying "him" or "her.")

Maybe one partner has a better job, is more outgoing, or is a natural leader. And the other partner may naturally move into a support role. If both are satisfied with that arrangement, there's nothing wrong with it. But for good balance to be maintained, they need to think of themselves as a team fulfilling different roles on the team—not as "her supporting him" or vice versa.

I have known pastors' wives who were especially skilled at being a "pastor's wife." It's a crucial role in a church that can involve counseling, encouragement, administration, music, wisdom, prayer, and a variety of other gifts. The pastor is obviously the "up front" person, the leader, and it's tempting to think of her supporting "his" ministry. But the finest pastor-couples I've known have always viewed it as "their" ministry. He's up front, she's behind the scenes (maybe), but there is balance in their relationship and in their ministry.

Earlier I talked about keeping score. There are different ways of doing this. When couples are in trouble, they start to play a zero-sum game. That is, if I get ahead, you must be behind. What's good for me is bad for you. You might see that as balance, but it works against a nurturing relationship.

As I write this, the Chicago Bulls are playing in the NBA finals. The Bulls' two finest players are Michael Jordan and Scottie Pippen, both league all-stars. These guys regularly score twenty or thirty points a game. Now maybe in the clubhouse, Pippen will tease Jordan if he happens to outscore him, but it will be all in fun. They do amass their personal statistics, but it would be absurd for them to compete against each other. *They are on the same team!* What's good for Jordan is good for Pippen, and they know it. That's why you see Jordan driving to the basket, drawing the defenders, and dishing off to Pippen for an easy jam.

Healthy relationships are like that. Both partners know they're on the same team. They work to support and encourage and inspire each other.

Here's another sports analogy. From my boyhood, I remember the ongoing rivalry between two track stars, Kip Keino of Kenya and Jim Ryun of the U.S. Both were world-class milers, shattering records with each race. It was not unusual for both to break the previous world record in the same race. That is, one of them would have his best time ever, what would be a new record—except he finished second.

But the interviews with those guys were precious. They were competitors, obviously. Both wanted to win. But each also appreciated the skills of the other, and they were glad for that head-to-head competition to spur them on. They pushed each other to do the best they possibly could, even if one of them had to finish second.

There was no zero-sum game with them. Good relationships, even among competitive people, have that aspect of encouragement, of challenge, of inspiration. When one wins, both win. That's the balance you need to have.

Chapter Fourteen

BOUNDARIES

My friend Tom Jones, whom I quoted earlier, was speaking with me at a conference. His subject was unconditional love. I spoke later in the day on relationship boundaries. He gave an excellent talk, saying many of the same things I said in chapter 12, delving into the Greek words and so on. "Unconditional love," he said, "looks for nothing in return but gives, gives, gives."

Following his talk, both he and I were beset by people saying, "I *did* give, give, give, and I got nothing in return. Now I'm a mess."

"I let my husband use me for years, and then he ran off with someone else."

"My boyfriend used to slap me around. Was I supposed to love him unconditionally in spite of that physical abuse?"

"That unconditional love stuff sounds good, but it just doesn't fly."

They needed to hear my talk about boundaries. Whenever we planned the conferences after that, we made sure to put the boundaries talk before the unconditional love talk. The two concepts need to be understood in tandem.

Unconditional love is a *personal* ideal. As an individual, you need to offer love with no selfish strings attached. Otherwise, it's not love; it's just manipulation or bargaining. Jesus made this point as He urged people to love their enemies: "If you love those who love you, what reward have you? Do not even the tax collectors do the same?" (Matt. 5:46). The tax collectors were viewed as the vilest of people. (Imagine that!)

Loving friends is easy because you know you'll get something back. But treating your enemies with love and kindness is much more difficult. They may sneer at you or spit on you or slap you around. To show love in those circumstances is a supreme challenge, but it can be done with God's help.

In a *relationship*, new rules enter the picture. Suddenly, I must be concerned not only with you and me but with "us." I may live my life in a self-giving, undemanding, sacrificial way. I may give my coat to the panhandler on the corner and my last dollar to the Salvation Army. But for a relationship to work, the love has to flow both ways. *For the good of "us,"* I must require you to show love to me as well. That takes boundaries.

Robert Frost was on to something profound when he wrote in his poem "Mending Wall," "Good fences make good neighbors." We tend to think that everything in a relationship should be free and open. No secrets, no closed doors, no boundaries. We don't like walls, but they're necessary for good relationships. Good fences make good partners.

I had a landlady who held a grudge against her neighbor because for ten years she had been mowing one strip of grass that belonged to that neighbor and never got a thank-you. My landlady was a gem. She would bring me food; she would pick up my mail when I was out of town. She was a giving person, but she was nasty toward the woman next door—all over one strip of grass.

"Maybe she thinks it belongs to you," I suggested once, and the thought stunned my landlady for a moment. Then she shook her head—no, no, that couldn't be.

They could have used a fence, a boundary. Then they would have known what was required and what was extra. They would have known the rules.

Any relationship between a man and a woman is a trinity—he, she, and it. It's a three-legged stool. To have an "it"—the relationship—both a "he" and a "she" are required. If they lose themselves, if they don't know who they are, if the relationship becomes exclusively about one partner or the other, the stool collapses. All three elements are necessary. How can you ensure that all three elements will be strong? You need to protect yourself, empower your partner, and define the relationship.

PROTECTING YOURSELF

Think of yourself as a liquid.

Picture this. A person walks inside on a hot day, gets a pitcher of water out of the refrigerator, and pours it—all over the kitchen table. Without a glass to hold the water, it's pretty useless—it's all over the place. The water needs *boundaries*. That's just the way liquid is.

So it is with a person. Some people pour themselves out for their partners. They lose all sense of who they are. Their whole identity is wrapped up in the other person. They have no boundaries. Sad to say, these people are like the water dripping on the kitchen floor. Without personal boundaries, they can't do much good—even for the people they're pouring themselves out for.

Bonnie was like that. You remember her story—going as a missionary to France, only to be used by her husband, then used by another man, and another. She gave up her personal boundaries. With low self-esteem to begin with, she kept trying to find her worth *in* the men. She served them. She made herself of use to them (and then complained that she was "used").

There are many people like her, so devoted to their partners that they will ditch their moral convictions, give up their rights, sever their friendships, quit their jobs, change their religion, and so on. They give up everything that makes them uniquely "them" to merge more closely with their partners.

How do you know if you lack personal boundaries? Symptoms may include the following:

- Being unable to keep secrets
- Talking at an intimate level on the first date
- Falling in love at first sight
- Falling in love with anyone who shows interest
- Thinking about someone all the time
- Violating your personal sexual standards
- Accepting food, gifts, or touching that you don't want
- Having the idea that your opinion doesn't matter
- Running yourself ragged for someone else's sake (especially when the person isn't lifting a finger)
- Letting others make decisions for you
- Letting others tell you how you feel
- Letting a partner decide who your friends will be
- Losing control so someone will take care of you
- Putting up with sexual or physical abuse
- Feeling obligated to do things for people you hardly know
- Finding it hard to say no, even when you know you should

You are not selfish to draw the line. You have to say, "Wait a second! This is who I am. I have certain rules, certain convictions, certain friends, certain requirements. I will meet you halfway. I will even go more than halfway. But you need to honor me for who I am."

We have seen this self-awareness in Sally and Laurie. They were able to grab the reins of their identity and to determine that they were worth more than they thought. They didn't need to sink themselves into addictive relationships. They could be worthy people as individuals.

We sometimes talk about people being users. They just want other people to serve them, to make their lives easier. Often, people with low self-esteem (and no personal boundaries) become us*ees*. And guess what? Usees attract users.

Karen told me, "I am a magnet for bad men." That's truer than she knows. As long as she operates without boundaries, seeking to serve every man she meets in any way she can, she will scare away the good men and attract the bad. It's a sad fact.

For many people who are being used in relationships, standing up and declaring their personal boundaries would put an end to those relationships. The users would not respect the new boundaries. They'd be off looking for someone else to use. That might be hard for the usee to take, but it's probably the best thing.

When I talk about boundaries, however, I'm not talking about rigid definitions. It's not "that's the way I am and I'm not going to change; take it or leave it, baby." Obviously, healthy relationships have some give-and-take. Your partner will affect you deeply, and you will affect your partner. To extend the liquid analogy, you might want to think of your "container" as a plastic bag full of water. It adapts to outside pressure, but it still contains and defines the liquid inside.

EMPOWERING YOUR PARTNER

In the language of addiction and codependency, we often speak of enablers. The enabler—often a spouse or girlfriend/boyfriend—helps an addicted person manage the addiction. Sounds great, doesn't it? It's not. The enabler helps the addict stay addicted.

When Sally's kids called in sick for her, they were enabling. Sure, they were trying to help. Mom needed to keep her job. But they were making it possible, at least for a while, for Sally to maintain her addictions and yet lead a rather normal life. And that kept her from seeking the help she needed—until it was almost too late.

Enablers make up for the effects of an addict's addiction. Enablers make excuses for the addict. Enablers are always forgiving, always trusting. They are often drawn into the addiction themselves.

What if you're not dealing with an alcohol or a drug problem? Can enabling still occur? In a way, yes. If your relationship is out of balance, if you would describe it as addictive, if you are being used by a user—you may be enabling your partner to treat you in unsatisfactory ways.

This behavior reminds me of a client who complained about regularly having to wait a half hour, an hour, or more for her partner to show up for a date. Yet every time she forgave him and agreed to go out with him again, she was enabling him to continue his inconsiderate tardiness.

But shouldn't you forgive? Yes, you should, but you should also hold your partner accountable for personal behavior. Remember that three-legged stool. You can forgive everything between "he" and "she," but the offending partner needs to know that the misdeed has harmed the "it"—the relationship. The rules have been broken. The relationship will not survive long if that behavior continues—even if you do offer forgiveness for any pain you sustained.

As I see it, the alternative to enabling is *empowering*. Instead of enabling your partner to continue in harmful ways, you seek to empower your partner to conquer these ways. Empowering happens not through excuses but through encounters, not through forgive and forget but through forgive and remind (of the rules of the relationship).

This concept is dangerous because you can take it only so far. You will not "save" your partner. If the relationship becomes all about teaching your partner how to treat you right, you're losing balance. The point is that by playing hardball with an errant partner, you *may* challenge the person to change. Or you may not.

Empowering means saying to your partner, "You are worth more than this. You are capable of better behavior." If your partner is caught up in a self-destructive addiction, you want to help that person recognize the value of the self and not destroy but restore. But relationships can be self-destructive as well for both partners. If there is abuse, physical or mental, the abuser is also abusing his own soul. Empowering is not saving but issuing a challenge rooted in the value of that person.

DEFINING THE RELATIONSHIP

Somewhere along the line, you need to decide what kind of a relationship you're going to have. This simple piece of communication may seem obvious, but many couples trip over it. I know guys who got married, expecting their wives to do the housewife routine, only to find that their wives were planning careers. A guy like that wants to bring home the bacon and be sure his wife cooks it. He doesn't expect a life full of microwavable platters.

The husband and the wife need to talk about who they are, what they want, what they need from each other. They need to define their relationship.

I talked with Rob about some of the frustrations in his dating life. "I was dating one woman—she was great—though it was still very casual between us," he said. "Except she had this bad habit of canceling out on dates at the last minute. I'd find a message on the answering machine saying she couldn't make it and she'd call later to explain. Well, she wouldn't call. So a week or two later I'd call her again, she'd be all nice and everything, and we'd go out a few times. And then she'd cancel again.

"We went through that whole cycle twice. Then one night I went to pick her up for a date, but she wasn't there. I was knocking at her door with fifty-dollar tickets in my pocket, but she wasn't there. That's when I decided I'd had enough. She was gorgeous, but I guess she knew it. I just couldn't let her treat me like that."

By going through the cycle twice, Rob and the woman were defining their relationship like this: she could cancel at the last minute and that was okay because Rob would forgive her and ask her out again. Those aren't good terms for a relationship. By refusing to call her now, Rob is protesting those terms. If she wants to go out with him, she will have to follow through on her commitments.

David, from our original group, told me how he was stringing along a young woman he was dating. She was crazy about him, and he was so-so about her. Then one day she erupted into a "you don't bring me flowers" speech. She was feeling unloved, unappreciated. She was trying to redefine the relationship: "I regularly show you how much I care for you, David, and you don't show anything in return. That has to change."

It changed for a while, but David realized that he did not want to have that kind of relationship with her. Ultimately, he broke up with her. That caused her some pain, but it was far better than being strung along in an undefined, ill-defined relationship. She forced his hand, defined her terms, and eventually freed herself from a potentially addictive relationship.

How can you define a relationship you're in?

1. *On your own, decide what you need from the relationship and what you're willing to give.* I don't want to make it sound too much like corporate negotiations, but you need to be prepared.

2. *Talk with your partner. Start by asking what the person wants from you in this relationship.* Your partner may not know. Or there may be things under the surface that are not mentioned outright.

3. *Discuss with your partner what* you *need.* See if you have any unreasonable requests (or if your partner does).

4. *If necessary, draw up an agreed set of rules for the relationship.* If your relationship is already in pretty good shape, the communication of the first three steps may be enough. But if things *have* to change, agree together on the terms of your relationship. Bringing flowers or stuff like that. Being on time. Not canceling out. Doing some things that *you* want to do. Going out with *your* friends sometimes.

Or there may be more serious issues. Stop hitting me. Stop doing drugs. Cool it on the sexual relationship. Do not belittle me in public.

5. *Be ready to leave if the rules are not followed.* Decide in advance. One strike? Two strikes? Three? How important are the rules to you? Are you willing to live by these relationship boundaries?

6. *Be aware that the relationship may not survive.* You aren't playing games. If you hold to certain boundaries, your partner may leave you, as David left the young woman. You may find that someone you want doesn't want you badly enough to play by your rules, as Rob discovered.

That may be painful for the moment, but it's the best thing for you.

It's possible that your partner will respond. You may restore your relationship on healthy, equitable terms. And that, of course, would be good, too.

So what does a healthy relationship look like when it has good boundaries? Both partners are aware of what they need from each other as well as what they need to give. They communicate freely when they are especially needy or feel used.

As best friends, they are willing to give 60, 90, or even 100 percent, but they also know that the relationship needs to be in balance. Each partner learns to lean on the other and be leaned on.

The "good fences" are there, but you'd hardly know it. There is no nit-picking, just a fair distribution of effort and love.

_____ *Chapter Fifteen* _____

CASE STUDY: CHRISTINE

Christine was always a good little girl. "Quiet and good," she says, looking back on her childhood. The attention in her early years was focused on her mother, who was frequently ill. Christine was an only child, but she didn't get the attention that usually goes with that status. Her father worked hard to care for her mother and to pay the medical bills. Christine stayed in the background, quiet and good, wanting to be of help but not sure what to do. She overheard an aunt say that Christine's birth may have intensified her mother's illness.

Her mother died when she was twelve.

By then, her father didn't know how to deal with her. He continued to work hard and paid little attention to Christine.

MARRIAGE AND AFTERWARD

Christine married a man very much like her father. Oh, at the time she thought he was gloriously different, but soon she fell into the same routine. He was a workaholic, she says, and she stayed home, quiet and good, eager to please, craving his attention. They were married twelve years, and he never knew where anything was in the kitchen. That was her domain.

Then he had an affair and left her. The man she had served for a dozen years, and dated six years before that, was gone.

Two years later, she found a new man. He was different, she thought. He was needy. He had been divorced only two weeks—his wife had just up and left—and he had an eleven-year-old daughter. Christine could identify with the girl who had just lost her mother. "I wanted to take care of her," she says simply. And the girl's father, John, needed caring, too.

Christine slid into her old role, giving and forgiving, quiet and good. John was frequently late for dates, "anywhere from a half hour to four hours late—and he wouldn't call." Christine was irked, but she put up with it. "He always had excuses. He said he didn't have a watch, so I bought him one. He wouldn't wear it. And he'd still be late," she states.

Like her father and like her husband, John was *unavailable*. He worked nights and weekends. Even when he was physically present, he wasn't emotionally with her. Christine was frustrated, but she was fighting the same old fight, struggling to win attention from a father figure.

John was restless. He said he wanted to date others. "Fine," said Christine. But he wouldn't. They dated four years and then were engaged. John was still restless. "I'm not ready to get married again," he would say. Not ready? After four years? But he was right. He had hooked up with Christine so soon after his divorce, he still had too many unresolved personal issues. Life was so easy with Christine serving him hand and foot, but was that what he really wanted?

Finally, John broke the engagement. He began dating someone else, whom he eventually married.

TRYING AGAIN

A year later, Christine fell in love again. "He walked in my front door, and my heart fell to the floor," she says. She had never believed in "love at first sight," but she felt it.

New man, same story. She observes, "He was much like my ex-husband, emotionally unavailable. I have never seen anyone stay in depression for that long." They dated two years and broke up.

"In every relationship I have," she says, "I seem to go after someone who won't give me the attention I want. He's unavailable in some way. I keep thinking it's me, that I have a problem, but I'm realizing that he just doesn't have it in him. That's the kind of man I choose."

Experts have suggested that when people look for partners, they often look for people like their parents—and try to change them. The childhood battles are fought all over again. This is true in Christine's case and in many, many other lives. The unavailable man syndrome is common. Our society has created many men who don't know how to give of themselves. Women like Christine get frustrated by it—*but they give in to it*. Their only strategy for success is to be "quiet and good" and servile and forgiving. They lose all personal boundaries and allow themselves to be taken for granted.

SEEKING AN ANSWER

After that two-year relationship, Christine came to see a female colleague of mine. Her presenting problem was actually a food addiction. In the wake of the latest romantic failure, she ate to numb her feelings. The counselor was able to confront the relationship addiction that was eating at her.

They began to talk about the kind of man Christine is attracted to. She has a natural attraction to good-looking men, but there's something else, too. She gravitates toward men who are emotionally unavailable. "If I'm immediately attracted to someone," she says, "I know there must be something terribly wrong with him." It's as if she longs for that challenge.

With her counselor's help, Christine has tried to change her ways. "I'm still probably going to have the tendencies," she says. "I'm still probably going to be attracted to the wrong people. But I'm learning not to judge a man for a potential relationship merely on the basis of whether I'm attracted to him. If I think he's a nice person and has a few marbles right in his head, I'll try to get to know him better."

As she does get to know a man, Christine has learned to focus on how he acts—not how he looks or what he says. "Look at his life," she tells herself. "How does he conduct himself?" She can sniff out a workaholic at ten paces. And she's learning to sense when a man is in denial about underlying problems. (That was the problem with John, who probably had not dealt with the deep-felt issues of his divorce. He was comfortable with Christine, but he needed to do some soul-searching before he could move on with a new relationship.)

ESTABLISHING NEW PATTERNS

Christine has also learned to establish good patterns at the beginning of a relationship. Shortly after she began counseling, she met a man who seemed interesting. She was not physically attracted to him, but he was intelligent and kind. Under her new rules, she decided to try to get to know him better.

She expressed her interest, and they went out a few times. She was very careful not to be too servile, as was her habit. "I gave nothing," she says, almost proudly. "If anything, I was too demanding." But she drew some affirmation from his enjoyment of her company. He liked Christine for who she was, not for the things she could do for him.

He was honest about dating someone else as well. That was fine. Christine was determined to go slow with the relationship. Ironically, the other woman gave him an ultimatum—all or nothing—and he decided to stop dating Christine.

Aw, shucks. There was none of the deep pain of previous breakups. Christine kept the relationship under control. She successfully played by her new rules.

A few weeks later, the guy called back: "Maybe I made a mistake. I really miss you. Maybe we could go out again."

What would the old Christine—the one with no boundaries—have said? "Sure! Whatever! I'm here for you!" And what did she actually say? Christine was friendly but firm: "When you make up your mind, call me."

Christine has learned to consult her friends and her counselor for advice about new relationships. She has a close friend whose dating life has paralleled her own. She now seeks this friend's opinion. Being accountable to her counselor keeps her from "love at first sight" attractions. They're great for the movies, but in real life they're fraught with difficulties.

As with so many relationship addictions, in Christine's case it comes down to self-image issues. Her troubles have stemmed from a fuzzy sense of who she is. If she's not gaining attention from a man, what good is she? She needs to learn that she has tremendous value all by herself. After a lot of work in counseling, she now says, "I think I deserve the best. I'm not going to settle."

MAKING A BREAKTHROUGH

Christine made a breakthrough when she restored her relationship with her father. They had seen each other on rare occasions, but Christine's counselor urged her to see her father again and try to resolve those issues of paternal love and attention seeking.

They had lunch together, father and daughter, and Christine poured out her soul. It was awkward—a man who had never been good at expressing his feelings, and a woman he was still somehow responsible for. Christine told of her failed relationships and the pain of each one. She was trying to be nice about it, but she could not be the "quiet and good" child any longer.

"One of the problems is," she stammered, "I think it comes down to . . . you never said you loved me."

The father squirmed in his seat. "Of course I did," he shrugged. "I mean . . . I do." At the time, Christine wasn't sure how much to trust that grudging confession. But as they got up to leave, her father moved over to her awkwardly and embraced her. "I really do love you," he said.

There was great healing in that moment. Christine has continued to meet with her father for lunch. And she continues to meet with her counselor. She is putting her life back together—on her terms.

EVALUATION

Once again, we see a childhood drama played out into adulthood. Christine's distant relationship with her father clearly affected her relations with men. She engaged in a form of self-sabotage by subconsciously seeking out men who were like her father. That type of man held an attraction for her, a challenge. And of course, there are many men like that, willing to be served but unavailable emotionally.

The food addiction was an interesting sidelight. Christine described it as a "numbing" thing. Her sensations of emotional pain over the constant rejection of the men she wanted were overcome by the pleasant sensations of taste. She might have sabotaged herself there, too.

The outlook for Christine is good. She is "finding herself," establishing a solid self-image. She is disciplining herself with food and with men, regaining control of her desires. She is reexamining her priorities, reappraising what she really wants in a man. And the renewed contact with her father is tremendously healing. It will not make all the childhood pain disappear immediately, but it will salve the wounds. Over time, the paternal relationship can help renew and restore Christine's sense of self.

One final note on these case studies. I have presented people in various situations. Some are in the middle of their struggles. They may have taken some steps toward recovery, but there's a long road ahead. Others, you might say, are healed. Their lives are back together. They seem healthy and happy.

Yet these "healthy" people know they could easily slip back to their addictive ways. They are like recovering drug or alcohol abusers who continue to describe themselves as recovering, even years later. Their attitude is, "I'm back on track now, but I know what I need to guard against. I will continue to be careful." This cautiousness is best for all of us, but it is especially important for those who are prone to unbalanced relationships. With caution they *can* recover, and they *can* have healthy new relationships.

_____ *Chapter Sixteen* _____

ADDICTION WITHIN MARRIAGE

People in addictive relationships often get married. Naturally, they carry all the controlling, the jealousy, the manipulation, the obsession, the abuse, the low self-esteem, and so on into the marriage with them. They think that marriage will solve these problems. It doesn't. It creates new problems and limits their options, specifically the option to walk away from the relationship.

A fellow counselor from another state told me of a couple she had been counseling. They were a classic case of addictions run wild. Both had serious self-esteem issues in their backgrounds. Both were extremely needy. Both had been through failed marriages and maintained custody of their children.

Their romance was quickly intimate. Their children first recognized the danger. Both partners were losing themselves in the new relationship—it was not healthy. Still, they were headed toward marriage. They consulted my colleague for premarital counseling.

181

One more thing: both partners had explosive tempers. It didn't take much to set them off. Their counselor found it hard to keep up. In one session they'd be cooing over each other, and in the next they'd curse and spit. They weren't just lovers' spats, either; they were out-and-out, I-never-want-to-see-you-again, I-despise-the-ground-you-walk-on brawls. But after a few weeks apart, they *had* to see each other, and they'd be back at it.

This love-hate cycle is a hallmark of addictive relationships. Driven by a compulsion to be with each other, they bring out the worst in each other and antagonize each other. Neither one is growing or helping the other grow. They seek relief for their deep emotional needs, but instead they reopen old wounds. It's "I'm nobody if somebody doesn't love me," but "somebody loves me only about a day or so before finding something terribly wrong with me."

Finally, in private sessions, both admitted that it was an unhealthy addictive relationship, and that they should cool it while they worked on their emotional needs. Good plan—except that within a month they were engaged to be married. "We just couldn't stand to be apart," they said.

Did the marriage change anything? What do you think? The last time I spoke with their counselor, she said they'd been fighting frequently. In their first year of marriage, one or the other had moved out three different times.

The addictive dating relationship had become an addictive marriage. Marrying each other only closed the back door. It added new ropes to tie them together. The marriage made finding *individual* healing much more difficult.

THE EXCEPTION

Every rule has its exceptions. I've been telling you that cold turkey is the way to go. If you are in an addictive relationship, get out. But here's the exception, and it's a huge one. *If you are married, try as hard as you can to keep the marriage together.*

You see, though I believe that relationship addicts need to stay away from the objects of their addiction, I believe even more in the sanctity of marriage. I take those vows seriously. In the wedding ceremony, we promise to be loyal "till death do us part" (or whatever they're saying nowadays). That's an oath to God and each other. It's not "till I no longer feel fulfilled in this relationship" or even "till my partner does something really bad."

I understand that we're not talking about casual divorce—"Oh, I'm bored with this one; let me try a new spouse." I understand that we're talking about emotional health, and that's serious. This is a very tough call, but I don't know how I can say anything other than this: if you're married, you've made a commitment to stay with that marriage.

As a Christian, I believe the Bible allows for divorce only in certain cases. It speaks specifically of adultery and abandonment by one's spouse as legitimate causes. (Not all Christians think alike on this issue, so I urge you to study it for yourself and consult your church leaders.) But in general, the Bible teaches, "What God has joined together, let no one separate."

Yet, in my work with Fresh Start Seminars, which conducts divorce recovery seminars in churches throughout the United States, I have met thousands of divorced people. I'm sure many of them have gotten divorced for reasons I would not approve, but I recognize their pain and their need for renewed emotional health. Many of them, I'm sure, were in relationships that might be considered unhealthy and addictive. Some of these people feel that divorce was the best of several bad options. I don't try to rewrite their history; I just try to help them take healthy steps toward the future.

But I also know many people who are enduring difficult marriages. Personalities aren't clicking anymore. Arguments abound. Each day is a struggle. I admire their tenacity, their desire to stay together even when it doesn't seem worth it. I believe that God will honor their faithfulness—somehow, somewhere.

If that is your situation, trapped in an unhealthy, addictive marriage, this chapter is a challenge. You have the unenviable task of climbing back up that slope, trying to regain your balance and your boundaries, and restoring the health of your relationship. Of course, many of the principles you have already read in this book will apply to your situation, but this chapter should offer extra insight.

DETACHMENT

Earlier I mentioned addiction as a matter of *attaching*. We attach our significance, identity, or pleasure to someone or something. In *Addiction and Grace*, Gerald May points out that our word *attach* comes from a French word meaning "nailed to." He comments, "Attachment 'nails' our desire to specific objects and creates addiction." If you are addicted to a specific person, think of yourself as nailed to the person. That person can't do a thing without your caring or worrying or wondering what the person thinks about you. Everything that you do is somehow nailed to that person as well. Will your partner approve? Will your partner notice? How does it compare to what your partner does? Will it make your partner happy?

You can see that in the fighting couple I just described. Even when they couldn't stand each other, they were obsessed with each other. Every action that one of them did was viewed as a statement to the other. In that context, a raised eyebrow, a yawn, or a certain tone of voice can spark an argument: "What did you mean by that?" They were clearly attached to each other, nailed tight, and the marriage just pounded in a few more nails.

Attachment is common among codependents (which is why the literature of Al-Anon and similar groups refers to it frequently). A codependent attaches his sense of significance to the welfare of the addicted partner. Every rise and fall in the addict's recovery deeply affects the codependent partner. The codependent's well-being is nailed to that of the addict. The result? Situations of caretaking in which the codependent makes decisions for the addict and thus limits the addict's responsibility. Attachment also leads to enabling behavior in which the codependent helps the addict manage the addiction and still lead a nearly normal life. The codependent may *think* that she is serving the best interests of the addicted partner, but at that level of attachment there is no distinction. Their interests are nailed together.

If you are in an addictive marriage, you need to begin a process of *detaching*. In severe cases, actual separation might be indicated, but that's not what I have in mind. (In cases of physical abuse, I recommend immediate separation. That cannot be tolerated.)

I'm talking about an emotional detachment, a process of finding yourself and releasing your partner. Ideally, it will free both of you for personal growth, and you might come together later on healthier terms. At the least, it will help *you* in *your* personal growth and keep you from going down the tubes of an unhealthy relationship.

Detachment is based on the belief that people are responsible for themselves. We can't solve problems that aren't ours to solve, and we can't make others change. We adopt a policy of keeping our hands off other people's responsibilities and tending to our areas of weakness. When people create problems for themselves, we need to allow them to face the consequences of their actions. We allow people to be who they are. It is their responsibility to grow, mature, and develop. We in turn accept our responsibility for personal growth.

If we cannot solve a problem and we have done all that we can, we learn to live with, or in spite of, that problem. Then we try to live happily—focusing heroically on what is good in our lives today and feeling grateful for that. We learn the important lesson that making the most of what we have multiplies our blessings.

DARLA

Let me tell you about one hero, my friend Darla. She probably would say that she hasn't done anything especially courageous, but I think she has. Darla is in the process of detaching from her husband for her growth and sanity, but she isn't divorcing him. She has weathered some hard times, and she still has an unhealthy marriage, but there's now a glimmer of hope. Darla met Stan at church about six years ago. Both were in their thirties, divorced and emotionally needy. Nothing was working out for Stan. He couldn't seem to keep a job, and he had various business schemes that always seemed to fail. Darla loved his "vulnerability." He was open and honest with her then. She, a caretaker by nature, had found someone to take care of. They were great friends. Only after friends suggested they'd make a great couple did they begin to consider a romance. After a lengthy friendship, they had a fairly short courtship. They already knew each other pretty well—or so they thought.

Both suffered from low self-esteem. He was rather bright in a street-smart way, but a learning disability had kept him from going to college. Each new business disappointment rankled him and stabbed at his pride. He bragged that he had learned far more in life than most people learn in college. He complained that the world was prejudiced against people without formal education. But his words masked a deep insecurity. Darla tended to agree with him, though she was college educated and had credits toward an MBA. She saw his brilliance in a way few others did. She could be his savior.

As you can see, there were some elements of an addictive relationship from the start. It was already a bit out of balance. The relationship was largely about *him*, helping him get on his feet economically, helping him unlock his potential. And Darla was more than happy to function that way.

Stan and Darla married and had children. She helped him start a business, and it prospered. They were able to buy a nice house in a nice community, and he began to hobnob with the business leaders of the community. Then he started other businesses, with some successes and some failures. Still, each failure stabbed at Stan; he had a lot to prove.

Darla noticed that Stan spent more and more time at his job. He was obsessed with his work. At home, he was too tired to do much of anything. He took up golf and became obsessed with that, devoting most of his weekends to improving his game. He was suddenly distant. They never talked as they used to.

He did not go out with Darla, nor did he help with the kids or the house. When Darla complained, he became extremely defensive. He claimed that he was still more communicative, more emotional, and more vulnerable than "most men," but then he'd pack up his things for a trip to some faraway golf haven. He worked hard, very hard, for Darla and the kids, he argued. He needed golf to unwind after a hard week of work.

It was as if he was protecting some precious treasure within him and Darla could not be trusted with it.

At first, Darla denied the problem. Stan was just going through a rough time, right? The crisis would blow over, right?

No, the problem continued, and Darla had to handle it. She worked closely with Stan in one of his business ventures in an effort to enter "his world." Maybe he would open up to her in that venue. It didn't happen. The tension carried over to the workplace, so Darla quit. Soon afterward she finished up her MBA work and got an entry-level job in the city.

Then she got angry. The more she thought about it, the angrier she got. How dare he treat her like that! How dare he put his job—and golf, for goodness' sake—ahead of his family! He was a tightwad with the family, but then he'd fly off on expensive weekend trips. She could never figure that out—but it made her mad. Yet whenever her anger erupted at him, he closed up more and became more defensive. He nearly left her at that point. Her anger was not saving the marriage.

So then depression hit her, physically as well as emotionally. She lost a lot of weight and couldn't sleep. "The whole thing is something like learning to live with cancer," she says, tracing the pattern of denial, bargaining, anger, and depression. "Eventually, I have to accept that this is the situation, and I need to respond to it in a healthy way."

Darla came out of her depression, although her anger still simmers from time to time. But she has done a good job of redeeming a bad situation. She works hard and tries to be a good mother and wife. She keeps the lines of communication open with her husband and yet does not pressure him. She is, in many respects, an independent woman. She has learned to fend for herself, to live her own life. She even entertains friends at home. Stan is invited to join them, but often he begs off.

There is a glimmer of hope in the counseling both are receiving. At least he has agreed to that. And there are faint signs that he is opening up. Darla has learned not to expect a lot. She knows there's a long, hard road ahead, but maybe things can change someday.

SURVIVING

If you feel yourself being drawn into a downward spiral, you *must* detach yourself from it. Break free. Let me repeat that I am not talking about divorce, but detachment may create distance. You are creating boundaries, walls that will protect your existence. You are moving to higher ground and challenging your partner to join you there.

It is not easy. Your partner probably will not like it. Your spouse may divorce you. But you must maintain a vision of wholeness—for yourself, for your relationship—that will keep you going.

And you must do everything with love. As you begin to break free, you will be tempted to hate, to hurt, to heckle, to hound. But put all of that aside. Act in love. It's a sober, tough love that creates distance between husband and wife. It's a prayerful, vigilant love that seeks healing for the relationship on healthy terms. It's a difficult love, but it's a strong love.

Dr. James Dobson touches on boundary setting in loving relationships in his book *Love Must Be Tough*. In speaking about an angry wife, he states,

> Look at it this way. Verbal bludgeoning never made anyone more loving or sensitive. You simply can't tear a guy to pieces and then expect him to meet your emotional needs. He's not made that way. Rather than attacking an unresponsive man and driving him away, there is a method of drawing him in your direction. It is accomplished by taking the pressure off him—*by pulling backward a bit*—by avoiding the worn out

accusations and complaints—by appearing to need him less— by showing appreciation for what he does right and for being fun to be with. Happiness (and self-fulfillment) is a marvelous magnet to the human personality.

Sometimes it is necessary to interject a challenge into the relationship in order to motivate a disengaged spouse. According to the "love must be tough" philosophy, a demeanor of self-confidence, mysterious quietness and *independence* is far more effective in getting attention than a frontal assault.

So how do you accomplish this? How can you pull backward a bit or detach from a bad situation? Besides the guidelines already mentioned throughout the book, here are some additional principles that may help you in your struggle.

1. Let go of your self-destructive impulses

Each of us has certain buttons that, when pushed, launch us into an orbit of self-hate. It doesn't take our spouses long to find out where they are. We have things we feel embarrassed about or insecure about. Some of us have certain temptations we find hard to resist.

When someone says the right thing (or the wrong thing, depending on how you look at it), we fight, we sulk, we feel guilty, we lose our resolve, we eat, we smoke, or we tumble back into an unhealthy relationship. We respond in different ways, but most of us are easily manipulated, especially by those closest to us.

You need to guard those buttons as carefully as if they launched nuclear warheads. Be ready with some self-talk to keep you out of orbit—"I will not feel guilty about that; I've been forgiven"; "I will not fight about this; it's not worth it"; "I'm not responsible for this person's life."

Recognize your partner's statement (or action) for what it is, a conscious or subconscious attempt to manipulate you, to reel you in, to maintain the relationship at its old addictive level. Don't let it happen. You are beyond that now. You're on a mission. You can let go of all that personal baggage now because "winning" in this relationship isn't important anymore. You're moving on to a new game.

2. Let go of your expectations, but verbalize your needs

Darla told me of a time when she was taking night classes once a week. She left Stan home with the kids. You might think that when she got home the kids would be put to bed and the place tidied up a bit. That's what she thought. But it never happened. The kids were clamoring, there were crumbs all over the couch, and Stan was sprawled out watching TV. She even dropped not-so-subtle hints about how she'd like Stan to put the kids to bed and so on. Still, nothing happened.

Eventually, she had to let those expectations go. Stan would never do what she wanted in the matter; she had to accept that. In so doing, she released herself from the continual disappointment she had been feeling. She had become angry and then depressed each time Stan failed her. She didn't need those feelings.

But she continued to verbalize her wishes and needs. She didn't shut him out entirely. If he wanted to run the marriage on reasonable terms, she was always ready to let him know what she desired. She would try not to nag him, but she would still communicate.

Holding it inside and pretending it didn't bother her would also be wrong. She needed to learn the balance of letting go of her expectations while verbalizing her needs. As she said, "Stuffing it only made me more angry and depressed."

At a church retreat for couples, spouses were asked to present each other with a "wish," something they'd like the partner to do for them. Darla wished to be taken out once for dinner, even at McDonald's, or an evening walk around the city—just the two of them. Stan agreed to do it sometime. She's still waiting. She brought it up a few weeks later. He grumbled something about not being able to afford a baby-sitter, and then he went out to buy new golf clubs.

Darla has learned to accept this response (or lack of one). She continues to present her wishes from time to time, but she refuses to get bent out of shape when they don't come true. (Perhaps you can see why I consider her attitude heroic.)

3. Let go of your control of your partner

This step is crucial, especially if you are a caretaker by nature. In that case, a substantial part of your identity is wrapped up in your partner's need for you. You regularly try to control, to change, to improve, or to affect your spouse's behavior. Your relationship may be largely based on that activity. And that's part of the problem.

Even if you're sure you are changing your spouse for the better, you need to let go. *Even if you fear your partner will fall apart without your control,* you need to give up that control. You are not responsible for your spouse. And as long as you control your partner's behavior, your partner doesn't have to take personal responsibility. Both partners will be better off if you stop controlling.

M. Scott Peck, M.D., author of *The Road Less Traveled,* echoed these thoughts when he reflected on much of the marriage counseling he has done over the years. In the lecture "Further Along the Road Less Traveled," he stated that "the problem with many couples is not too much separateness, but rather too much togetherness." He went on to explain that a healthy relationship for those who are out of balance is many times a matter of "backing away from each other." He shared with the crowd that about five years into his marriage, he and his wife "hit bottom." He got angry with his wife, began to withdraw from her, and finally started not to care about her so much. She reciprocated by not caring about him.

As Dr. Peck put it, "You know what I mean when I say we stopped caring about each other? I mean that I gave up trying to change and control her life, and she gave up trying to change or control me. And our marriage has been steadily improving ever since!"

This concept reminds me of a children's toy I ran across years ago. It's a cylinder made from flexible interwoven strips. I believe it's called Chinese handcuffs. If you put your fingers in on both sides and pull as hard as you can, it tightens so that you can't get out. Only when you push in does the gizmo relax its grip. There are many relationships in which people are trapped because they're pulling so hard in one direction: "If only you become what *I* want you to be, we can have a great relationship." Their desperate attempts to control the other person, even though they mean well, trap them in a dismal situation. But when they relax, allowing the other person to make choices, they can escape from the grip of that relationship addiction.

It sounds easy. But it's hard when you're in the middle of it. It would be one thing to walk away from the relationship, but to stay in the marriage and renounce your control—that's a challenge. You need to keep a check on your attitudes:

- "I will care about my spouse, but I will not caretake."
- "I will inspire, but I will not enable."
- "I will communicate without nagging."
- "I will be humble but not self-destructive."
- "I will have a servant's heart, but I will observe certain healthy boundaries."
- "I will allow my spouse to disagree with me; I will not give in just to keep the peace."

Darla's efforts to improve her relationship with Stan were met with more defensiveness. She was there with her college education (and a minor in psychology) trying to define the relationship on her terms. He resented her attempts to control things. He was afraid of losing himself to her control. He feared that he would become just a product of her caretaking efforts. In his business and on the golf course, he could be his own man.

So Darla had to back off. She had to let him be the way he wanted to be. She had to renounce her control of him. That was the only way he would ever feel secure enough to open up to her again. It might never happen—it hasn't happened yet—but it's also the only way she could get on with her life.

4. Pick your battles

This extremely practical point must be added to this supply of psychological advice: "Let go"; "Renounce." Sounds good, but what happens in the trenches when Johnny needs new shoes and your partner has just spent your last dollar on a new nine iron?

In the gritty day-to-day details of life, both spouses need to decide some things together. There will be conflicts. You will *need* to control some things for the survival of your family or yourself.

So pick your battles. Don't make a federal case out of every disagreement. Let a lot of stuff slide. But when there's an issue that your spouse *must* address—behavior *has* to change—address it. Make your case as best you can.

Haggling over every detail will create a warlike atmosphere, and it will draw you farther into the downward spiral. But if you choose your spots carefully, you can accomplish most of what you need to while staying free of overentanglement.

5. Find your identity

Psychologists have noted that *security* and *significance* are basic factors of every person's identity. When they are shaken, our lives are in turmoil.

It is natural for us to find these elements in our spouses. There is a sense of emotional security in knowing "I am loved by this person" or at least a practical security in knowing "I have someone to be with." We can find significance in recognizing that "I am important to this person" or "I affect this person's life in a major way."

The process of detaching involves finding your security and significance *apart from* your relationship with your spouse. Who are you on your own? How would you manage by yourself? What good are you without a spouse to care for? These are hard questions, but you must ask them—and answer them.

Please understand that this is not my typical marital advice. No, for most couples, security and significance are found in their marriage relationship. And that's the way I believe it should be. But what are Darla and other women like her to do when they get little or no affirmation from their spouses?

As I've said, I work regularly with people who are newly divorced. Many of them are literally in a daze. Their foundational sense of security and significance is shaken. I remember having that feeling when my wife left me. You don't know who you are.

Detachment within a marriage takes you through that process more slowly to prepare you against the impending storm. As you consider these basic questions and find new answers, you will lessen your unhealthy dependence on your spouse.

Try this idea. Get a sheet of paper and write ten answers to this question: Who am I? You might include talents, temperaments, interests, relationships, faith, opinions, background, work, and so on. Now go back through that list and cross out everything directly related to your spouse. If you needed to be totally on your own, would these things apply?

You're probably left with eight or nine things that describe you. YOU. Just you. Not as wife of So-and-so or husband of What's-her-name. This could be the beginning of an awareness of yourself. You can think in the singular case now. You can develop your individual identity.

Consider questions like these:

- What is my political persuasion? Do I favor Democrats, Republicans, or Independents?
- What is my favorite TV show or movie or play?
- What is the best feature of my personality?
- If I got $300,000 in the mail today, what would I do with it?
- When have I felt closest to God?
- If I had a year to travel, where would I go?
- What do I think is the greatest need of our country today?

Obviously, these are just starter questions. But if you can answer them for yourself, without checking your spouse's opinion, that's good. Remember our case study with Sally? She was in an unhealthy marriage for twenty-three years. Her husband gradually chipped away at her self-esteem to the point that she had no opinions of her own. She didn't know she could have a favorite TV show. If you gave her $300,000, she'd give it to her husband to handle.

Detachment involves finding yourself, getting to know who you are.

6. Find something to do

Shore up your sense of significance by getting a job if you don't have one. Or volunteer for a church or charitable organization. Or take up an artistic pursuit or hobby.

Darla finished her degree and got a job. She was making an attempt at detachment. Stan accepted it, largely because they could use the money, but he resented it, too. This reaction is fairly common. As you begin to establish your own identity and activities, your spouse may feel threatened. You are beginning to break free, and that puts the relationship on unfamiliar turf. But stay with it. You need to realize that you can have significance outside the marital relationship.

7. Develop new friendships

Friends can give you emotional security. If all else falls apart, they will be there for you. Friends also encourage you in the difficult times, and as you know, there are many difficult times. Friends can critique you as well. If your judgment is faulty, if your plans are foolish, if your attitudes are out of line, good friends will tell you so (especially if you give them permission).

As I've said earlier in this book, addictive relationships have a way of folding in on themselves. The partners focus on each other and let other friendships slide. Or one jealous partner discourages or forbids the other from having outside friendships. Part of finding yourself involves finding your own friends.

As Darla got increasingly frustrated with Stan, she turned to friends at work and church for emotional support. Developing friendships was an essential part of her return to health. She cautions, however, that it's important to find friends who understand your goals. Several people she confided in were quick to say, "Dump him!" They didn't understand her commitment to the marriage. She needed people to help her through the process of becoming a whole person while staying in the marriage.

8. Become self-sufficient in practical matters

A friend told me about his grandmother, who lost her husband when they were both about sixty. For forty years, she had relied on him for the practical matters of running the home. Oh, she took care of the *inside* of the home—cooking and cleaning—but he wrote the checks, ran the errands, and so on. After his death, she was at a loss. She could not get a credit card. She had a hard time dealing with the insurance company. She had to learn to drive all over again.

Many wives are like that today. They are totally dependent on their husbands for financial matters. On the other hand, many husbands are at a loss when it comes to the upkeep of the home and child rearing. (Forgive me for proliferating the sexual stereotypes, but many homes have adopted these traditional roles.)

It would help you to learn some practical matters. If you were suddenly single, what would you need to know to function on your own? Darla got a job and began to make a modest living of her own so she wouldn't be dependent on Stan's rising and falling business interests.

You may be thinking, *Preparing for divorce . . . that's all this is.* Believe me, that's not my intention. But it is all a part of *detachment*. When one partner is unhealthily dependent on the other, the dependencies need to be changed. In the ways I've just listed, you may be able to let go of some things that are messing up the relationship and find your personhood.

The ideal is that you and your partner might eventually come together on different terms, more healthy terms. A great amount of healing and change will have to take place first, but there is always hope.

If *you* have chosen this heroic route, I commend your choice. You have not chosen the seemingly easier route—to start over with someone else. Instead, you have chosen to honor your commitment in marriage. I hope that you will be able to find yourself and then to discover a new, healthier marriage.

_____ *Chapter Seventeen* _____

ADDICTION IN A SAME-SEX FRIENDSHIP

Though this book has focused primarily on romantic relationships, I have also mentioned other environments for addictive relationships. Obviously, a few of the details of the symptoms and the prescription for recovery will be different when we take a look at same-sex relationships, but most of the same principles apply. Still, the uniqueness of these situations deserves mention. Let's begin with a story of two close friends.

Cara and Kim are both twenty-five years old. They became fast friends in high school and have talked to each other at least once a day ever since. Both have boyfriends, and they often double-date. Even when they don't double, they regularly compare notes about their dates.

At one point a few years ago, Kim struck up a friendship with a new secretary in the office where she worked. They often took lunch breaks together. Every so often she mentioned to Cara that "Betty said this" or "Betty did that." Cara became quite jealous, though she wouldn't admit it at first, even to herself. But she feared that Betty was taking her place as Kim's best friend, and she didn't know how she would survive without that friendship.

Subtly at first, but then more openly, Cara signaled her disapproval of Kim's new friend. She began to change her schedule to have lunch with Kim more often, and she warned Kim that Betty might be "using" her to get in good with people at the office. Kim eventually cut back on her lunches with Betty, but Cara still was unhappy about that friendship. Ultimately, Cara found a new job for Kim near where she worked.

Kim was concerned about Cara's jealousy, but she enjoyed Cara's friendship and didn't want to threaten it. Earlier this year, Kim took an impulsive weekend trip to New England. When she returned, Cara was furious.

"You didn't tell me a thing about it," Cara charged. "I called you all weekend. I thought you died or something. I was worried sick." Even when Kim explained how sudden it all was, Cara scolded her for not letting her help plan the weekend and for not inviting Cara along.

Kim felt guilty. She apologized profusely and bent over backward in the next few weeks to be a good friend to Cara.

OTHER CONSIDERATIONS

Kim and Cara are not lesbians. There is no sexual or romantic involvement. It is true that some homosexuals develop that kind of emotional dependency, but that does not necessarily indicate the friends are gay. (Certainly, many other issues are involved in homosexual relationships. I will not address them here.)

Emotional dependency is more common in female friendships but not exclusive to them. I once had a male friend who attached himself to me and grew too dependent on our friendship. He was not gay, just emotionally dependent, but it was an unhealthy situation, and I had to ease out of it. Still, in our culture, the deepest emotional bonding seems to occur among women.

(Male-female friendships could develop an emotional dependency without being romantic, but that's rare.)

DEFINING THE PROBLEM

Where do you draw the line? Where does a good friendship go astray? Is it wrong to call a friend every day? Is it wrong to compare notes about your love life?

Go back to chapter 4 to check out the characteristics of addictive relationships. The same principles apply. In the case of Kim and Cara, we see a friendship that's definitely out of balance.

We see it first in the *exclusive* nature of the friendship. It's a closed circle—no one else can get in. Even the boyfriends are on the outskirts, it seems. When the exclusivity is breached, *jealousy* rears its ugly head. Powerful negative feelings arise, even if they're irrational.

In a healthy friendship, Cara would rejoice with Kim in her discovery of a new friend. She might try to befriend Betty, suggesting that the three of them go out together. Healthy relationships are *inclusive*. The more, the merrier.

Hidden beneath the jealousy is a *lack of trust*. Cara does not trust that Kim will continue to be a friend to her if she has other friends or if she goes off with her boyfriend somewhere outside Cara's control. This lack of trust often comes from *poor self-esteem*. If I don't believe that I'm worth befriending, I'm afraid that you will run to a better friend.

That poor self-esteem also shows up in a *lack of boundaries*. As I said in chapter 14, good fences make good partners. Good fences make good friends. I need to know where I end and where you begin. What are my responsibilities, and what are yours? What privacy do I have? What decisions can I make by myself?

Cara trampled down whatever boundaries Kim may have had. Kim could not go off for a weekend without asking Cara to help plan it and maybe go along! Kim could not make other friends. And Cara found Kim a new job, exercising her control in that way, too. It was as if Cara needed to live Kim's life for her.

So far, I'm making Cara seem like a real villain. But Kim is a willing accomplice. I recognize some aspects of a caretaker in Kim. She sees that Cara needs her, and she responds to that. (Note that the new secretary needed a friend in her new office, and Kim rushed to help.) Kim is not as directly dependent on Cara as Cara is on her, but she responds to Cara's dependency. Cara lays a guilt trip on her, and Kim feels guilty.

Cara, in effect, says, "I needed you, and you weren't there for me."

How does Kim respond? She *could* say, "That's not true. I've always been there for you, but your demands are unreasonable. I needed to get away."

But no. She says, "You're right. I'm sorry. It won't happen again." She allows Cara to erase the boundaries between them. Apparently, certain needs within Kim are met when she gives in to Cara. She feels responsible for Cara's well-being, and so she allows Cara to invade her life. If she didn't do this, she would be a bad person—or so she thinks.

Both would be healthier if they could put up walls. Cara needs to get a life of her own and to be happy with that. The best thing Kim could do for Cara is to withdraw and to force Cara into self-sufficiency.

HOW TO FIND HEALING

How will these two achieve a healthy friendship? Maybe they can't. Based upon what you've read in the rest of this book, you won't be surprised that if the relationship is far out of balance, I would recommend a complete cold turkey separation. As with any addiction, moderation is not an effective strategy. The best thing for Cara and Kim would be to withdraw from each other for at least a year. It would be hard to do and painful, but it's the best way.

If that is impossible, a backup strategy would be something like what I suggest for people in addictive marriages: detachment. If they must keep some sort of friendship in place, they should at least put some distance between them. They should set up some boundaries and make some rules.

I might suggest that Kim and Cara limit their phone calls to once or twice a week rather than every day.

Staying away from conversation about their boyfriends might also be healthy. (I suspect that the romantic relationships may be stunted by the constant interaction between the two friends.)

Further, I would urge both friends to be sensitive about guilt mongering. Cara should try to recognize when she is laying a guilt trip on Kim, and she should avoid doing it. Kim should recognize it, too, and refuse to buckle under.

I would also recommend that both friends get involved in a new activity that they keep private from each other. Each person could grow apart from the other's control.

Such measures may or may not get the friendship on a healthier course. If the dependency is mild, this may be the way to go. The friendship could continue on healthier terms. But if there is a serious emotional addiction, I would recommend a complete break. I know that splitting up best friends sounds harsh. But in cases like that, the relationship has grown beyond friendship into an unhealthy attachment.

Besides distancing from each other, Kim and Cara need to take a serious look at why the relationship got so far out of balance in the first place. Their relationship is a symptom of a deeper problem. Without each other, they have treated only the symptom. They are very likely to replace that missing friendship with someone else. More specifically, I would suspect that their boyfriends would soon replace that missing need, and a romantic addiction could easily develop. Therefore, any correction of an addictive relationship must be accompanied with a commitment to address the issues that led to the problem.

A healthy friendship becomes a resource for personal growth. For persons prone to addictive relationships, friendships are essential for accountability, they provide affirmation and support, they teach about trust and unconditional love, and they become a springboard for all other relationships.

Characteristics of healthy relationships were contrasted with those of addictive relationships in chapter 4. Let me review some of the characteristics as they apply specifically in a friendship.

1. Friends get together because they enjoy each other's company—not because they feel any compulsive need or guilt when they don't see each other.

2. Friendships are mutual and reciprocal. They are not driven by a need to rescue but instead contain elements of mutually helping each other through support and encouragement.

3. Friendships are honest and objective. Friends can feel free to share their hearts with each other and know that they will not be judged. One also is assured that the other will give objective feedback, not be tainted with an overly negative perspective or blinded by rose-colored glasses.

4. Friends enjoy the company of others. Sure, there are times when they want to be alone with each other, but in general, friendships are not exclusive.

5. Friends trust each other. They are not jealous when they hear about other friends.

6. Friends are whole people who enjoy each other and are not dependent on each other.

7. Friends build each other up. The relationship is growing and supportive. They do not punish, shame, or in any way weaken the other person. Their relationship is not a love-hate cycle but a slow, steady, growing friendship.

_____ *Chapter Eighteen* _____

FAMILY RELATIONSHIPS

Even in family settings, the most basic human relationships, attachments can become unhealthy. True love can become emotional dependency. And it can go both ways—a parent dependent on the child, or a child clinging too long to parents. We'll talk first about a parent's overattachment to a child.

PARENT-CHILD DEPENDENCY

At the beginning, there are no boundaries between a mother and a child. The child is physically part of the mother's body, wholly dependent. After the birth, the baby remains dependent, though obviously less attached in a physical way. Both father and mother care for the child, feeding her, clothing her, and making virtually all of her decisions. As the child grows, he develops a will of his own. All parents know that the child's will does not always conform to the parents' will. But in most cases, parents stay in control up to the teen years when the child assumes more

203

and more responsibility for herself. A problem occurs when parents fail to let go. They try to maintain control of their child's life well into adulthood. That control needs to be released.

The goal of parenting is to create independent, healthy individuals. It's a give-and-take process that encourages the growth, decision making, and independent thinking of the child. Obviously, some measures of independence that would be fine for a seventeen-year-old would be inappropriate for a twelve-year-old. But healthy child rearing always moves in the direction of independence. Effective parents are always preparing to let go.

When a parent continues to "baby" a child, something's wrong. When a parent makes decisions for an adult child or imposes opinions on every aspect of the adult child's life, that parent is not letting go. If a parent is unable to accept the independence of a grown child, an unhealthy addiction is at work.

In his lecture "Further Along the Road Less Traveled," M. Scott Peck observed an interesting paradox. He stated, "Children who grew up in warm, nurturing, loving homes usually had relatively little difficulty in leaving those homes. Whereas children who grew up in homes filled with backbiting, hostility, coldness, and viciousness often had a great deal of trouble leaving such homes."

Dr. Peck went on to point out that this observation, though illogical, is nonetheless a reflection of the fact that children from dysfunctional families become enmeshed in the dysfunctional system and then view the world as a hostile, uncaring place. Parents who raise their children in a healthy environment teach them independence and what Dr. Peck called separateness. Then as they grow up, they look forward to the challenges of the outside world, and they are much better prepared to face that world. He concluded by saying, "Ultimately, it is the goal of the parent to help the child separate."

A case in point

Connie, a recent client of mine, comes by to talk about her scoundrel of a husband and why she has decided to leave him.

But as she tells of her troubles, she keeps referring to her parents' opinions. Whether she admits it or not, she is controlled by them, though she is well into her thirties.

Her parents continue to pass judgment on her decisions. And Connie, with a childhood longing for Daddy's approval, lets their judgments affect her decisions. She complains that they baby her, that they hold her back from reaching her potential, and yet she is irrationally drawn to them. She lacks the strength to defy their opinions.

It's interesting to see how these things get passed from one generation to the next. Connie has a teenage daughter who is considering going off to college. Connie is emotionally devastated by this prospect, and she is doing all she can to make sure the daughter stays home. "It's not safe," she tells her daughter. "Wait until you're older. You'll get lonely being so far from home." The truth is, Connie fears her own loneliness, her own lack of safety. She finds a certain security in her attachment to her daughter, and she can't let go.

We often see this tendency among mothers whose children are leaving the nest. Our culture (at least part of our traditional culture) has conveyed the message that a woman's sole value is in motherhood. When the children are no longer around to be a mother to, a mother experiences a major identity crisis. She can lose her sense of significance. What does she do now? Some just try to keep mothering their children to an unhealthy point.

The tendency is less severe among fathers, who often find their significance elsewhere. But they sometimes experience a crisis of control. A father of grown children can be like the corporate president whose company goes bankrupt. He's not in charge of anything anymore; all he can do is to be a consultant.

A single friend joked that whenever she visits her parents, her mom gives her food and her dad gives her advice. "Without fail," she said. "It happens every time."

This is not necessarily unhealthy. But these trends can reach a point where they indicate an unhealthy addiction to the children. How do you know when it's a problem?

Symptoms

When a parent seeks to *control the life* of a grown child, it's dangerous. It's one thing to give advice. It's another to get upset when the advice is not followed. It's even worse to apply emotional or financial or practical pressure to assure that the advice is followed. Like a spouse, a parent often knows the emotional buttons to push.

Also watch for *role reversals*. If a parent gets too emotionally dependent, the child may actually take on a parental role. The child is forced to make decisions about the relationship: "Yes, you may go shopping with me. No, I don't have time to talk now." To maintain health, the child is forced to determine the bounds of the relationship.

And that's another danger sign: *boundary violations*. Parents sometimes get too enmeshed in their children's lives. They must know everything the children are doing, and some need to be involved in it all, too. They may invade their children's privacy in other ways. They may identify with their children too much, living life vicariously through them. As with any other relationship, they need to build healthy boundaries—this is your life, this is mine.

Restoration

How do you restore the relationship? I would treat it like an addictive marriage. That is, cold turkey is not the best way to go. If you can redefine the relationship on healthier terms, do it.

If you are a parent and you are unhealthily enmeshed with your child's life, you need to *learn to let go*. You may have to undertake mental reorientation. You need to enjoy the independence of your child. Remember, that's the goal of parenting. Recognize your attempts to cling to your child, and try to talk yourself into letting go. Your child will make mistakes. You cannot spare a child the pain of those mistakes. It is only through such mistakes that a child learns.

A mother of a physically disabled child was talking with a friend. The child was standing nearby, playing, and he fell—not seriously. The mother looked on as the boy struggled to get back up. With his disability, it wasn't easy, but eventually, the boy was back on his feet.

The friend was astonished. "Why didn't you help him?" she asked the mother.

"I did," the mother replied.

It takes the wisdom of Solomon sometimes to know when to step in and when to back off. Parents have a difficult task. But if you are aware of an unhealthy enmeshment with your child, learn the wisdom of that boy's mother. You help the most by letting your child do it himself.

Decide on boundaries and observe them. Discuss them with your child, or just adopt them. You might limit the time spent with your child or on the phone. You might limit the advice you give or even the financial aid you offer.

Learn your child's emotional "hot buttons" and stay away. As a parent, you can destroy your kid with a word. You have that power. You know instinctively how to cut to the core of that person. Part of healthy boundary observing is training your instincts to stay away from sore spots. Talk with your child about what they are.

Get a life. Seriously, as you develop your skills, interests, and personality outside of parenting, you will have less need to invade your child's life.

Strategies for the adult child

What do you do if you are the grown child of a parent who will not let go?

Talk about it. Tell your parent of your need for independence. Work through the steps listed above, especially the boundary setting.

Sidestep the guilt trip. A parent who doesn't understand your needs may try to instill guilt. Don't buy it. You are trying to save a relationship—just as a spouse might work to save a marriage. You are merely recognizing that the current state of affairs is not healthy. You are trying to establish the ground rules for a new, healthy relationship. You are actually trying to help your parent do a better job of parenting you. It may seem selfish, but in the long run it's the best thing for your parent as well.

Detach if necessary. If your parent refuses to abide by proper boundaries, you may need to distance yourself. Move away, or stay away for a time. Or even if you must maintain contact, limit the ways in which you cooperate with parental control. You don't have to tell him everything. You don't have to seek or accept her advice. The goal is always to come back together at some future point in a more healthy way. But even if that doesn't happen, the individuals involved need to find emotional health.

CHILD-PARENT DEPENDENCY

Reverse the fields. Let's talk about when a child will not let go of her parents. It is a special problem when it affects a marriage.

Rick and Nancy came to me for counseling. "Nancy sees or calls her mother every day," Rick complained.

"What's wrong with that?" Nancy replied.

"But it's all the time," Rick explained. "She'll call her from work. Then she'll stop by on the way home from work. Then she'll call her after dinner and chat for an hour or more. I sometimes think her mother's more important to her than I am."

"That's ridiculous," Nancy said, rolling her eyes.

Rick went on. "About six months ago, Nan got a promotion at work. Great news, right? She comes home, says, 'Hi, hon,' and heads right for the phone. I overhear her telling her mother about her promotion. That's how I found out about it."

Nancy was shaking her head. "You don't understand."

"It seems like any decision we make has to be approved by her mother," Rick added. "We can't just decide to go on vacation. We have to check with Mom for the dates and destination."

"She had been to Cape Cod and didn't like it, that's all," Nancy explained. "She said it was better in the fall."

But Rick was on a roll. "The worst of it is when her mother gets me on the phone and says, like, personal stuff that Nancy hasn't even talked with me about."

"Like what?" Nancy challenged.

"Like, 'So, Rick, Nancy says you haven't been very energetic in bed lately. What's wrong? You working too hard?'"

"She did not say that!"

"She most certainly did!"

You get the idea. A week before I saw them, they had had an awful fight (imagine that!), and Nancy walked out. Guess where she went? Mother's.

In private counseling a week later, Nancy told me that if she had to choose between Rick and her mother, she'd choose Mom. "After all, I've known him only four years, and I've known her all my life."

Evaluation

In my opinion, Nancy has an unhealthy, perhaps addictive, relationship with her mother. There are *a lack of independence in decision making* and an obvious *violation of personal and marital boundaries*. In addition, the relationship seems to be rather *exclusive*, shutting out Nancy's husband.

The book of Genesis offers ancient wisdom on the subject. Adam calls Eve "bone of my bones and flesh of my flesh" (Gen. 2:23), and the writer adds the comment: "Therefore a man shall leave his father and mother and be joined to his wife, and they shall become one flesh" (Gen. 2:24).

For both men and women, the leaving of parents is an important step toward solid marriages and other healthy relationships. It doesn't mean you never talk to them or you disdain what they say. But your priorities change. You develop new loyalties.

Nancy and the many people like her need to adopt the same strategies we have been talking about—*detachment* and *boundaries*. With proper communication, joint effort, and a firm decision to change, the unhealthy child-parent relationship can turn into a healthy friendship with appropriate limits.

CONCLUSION

In this book, you have met several people, all of whom have struggled with unhealthy relationships that would be considered addictive in some way. Sally, Christine, Scott, and the others had unique situations—but I'm sure you recognized some common threads throughout.

That was the secret of the original group I convened in chapter 1. Each member had a story. But all had similar sufferings. Each person could say to the others, "I know what you're going through. I don't know *exactly* what you're going through, but I've felt something like it."

The problem with a book like this is that I don't know *exactly* what you're going through. I don't know why you picked up this book. I have no idea of the impact it will have in your life. Your situation is unique.

And yet you can learn from Sally, Christine, and the others. Their stories, and the principles presented here, may help you cope with your particular problems. It's up to you, though, to sift through the information. You have to toss out what doesn't apply and hold on to what does. It's up to you to draw up your plan of action based on the principles you have found here.

THE GOD FACTOR

There are two kinds of people reading this book: those who depend on God in their day-to-day lives, and those who don't. I'm tempted to say "religious" and "irreligious," but it really has very little to do with the forms followed. It's a matter of the liveliness of faith. For some, God is a daily guide, a teacher, and a comforter. Others don't think much about God in their regular activities.

The first group is saying, "Why doesn't this book say more

about faith in God? God has power to fix these problems for people!"

The second group is saying, "Why does this book talk about God so much?"

Let me try to answer both groups.

I believe that God heals people. Sometimes He defies all medical expectations and works a miracle. But I still see a doctor when I'm sick because I believe that God uses *natural* processes of healing and doctors are trained to recognize and enhance the natural processes.

The same holds true for emotional healing. There are natural processes by which people are healed. Detachment. Renewed identity and self-esteem. Balance and boundaries. All of them can help people break free from unhealthy dependencies. To say, "Just trust in God and He will make it all better," is to ignore the processes by which He makes it better.

And yet I do believe in miracles. I sincerely thought Sally would die from her addictions, but here she is in front of me, happy, confident, and free. That's a miracle.

Laurie was in the pits of despair over her failed relationship with her boss. She talks about learning to depend on God. She praises God for bringing her back to health. That, too, is a miracle.

Twelve-Step programs, starting with Alcoholics Anonymous, have recognized the need to depend on a Higher Power. Part of the healing process is to come to the end of your strength and to reach out for divine aid. I've seen that happen in case after case after case.

Churches expend a lot of effort trying to help people become holy. Unfortunately, *holiness* has taken on some negative connotations. In popular imagery, a holy person is one who has no fun and doesn't want anyone else to have fun. But linguistically, *holiness* is essentially the same as *wholeness*. Yes, God wants us to be holy (through His work in our lives, not our efforts). He also wants us to become whole, and He wants to help us with that.

If you are feeling partial these days, as if a chunk of you is missing, if you seem to have lost the part of you that makes sound decisions or enjoys healthy relationships, if you are craving the love you never got as a child or desperately reaching for a mystery ingredient that our society keeps saying you need, the *true* Higher Power, God, can make you whole. Having a relationship with Him is a matter of surrendering your life to Him, trusting that He knows what is best for your life. He is the only One who can fill the void of an empty life. No relationship, no lover, and certainly no addiction can do that.

Miracles happen, even today. Recovery *is* possible in your life. Just ask Sally or Christine or Laurie or Scott or . . .

ABOUT THE AUTHORS

Dr. Thomas Whiteman is the founder and president of Life Counseling Services in Paoli, Pennsylvania, and president of Fresh Start Seminars, a divorce recovery program for children and adults. Fresh Start conducts over fifty seminars a year throughout the United States on divorce recovery and related issues. Whiteman is also the author of *Innocent Victims* and the coauthor of *The Fresh Start Divorce Recovery Workbook* (with Bob Burns) and *The Fresh Start Single Parenting Workbook* (with Randy Petersen). He and his wife, Lori, have three children, Elizabeth, Michelle, and Kurt.

Randy Petersen has written books on singleness, worship, and church history, as well as plays and small-group curriculum for youth and adults. He is involved in local theater as an actor, director, and acting teacher. A former editor of *Evangelical Newsletter*, Randy has led several church singles groups.

For more information on seminars, counseling services, and other resources, contact the Fresh Start office:

Fresh Start Seminars
63 Chestnut Road
Paoli, PA 19301
1-800-882-2799